NURSERY-KINDERGARTEN WEEKDAY EDUCATION IN THE CHURCH

The Cooperative Series

This book has been developed through the cooperative efforts of many denominations seeking through an interdenominational agency, the Cooperative Publication Association, to provide publications of sound educational value and practical usefulness.

JOSEPHINE NEWBURY

Nursery-Kindergarten Weekday Education in the Church

published for the

COOPERATIVE PUBLICATION ASSOCIATION
by John Knox Press

Richmond, Virginia

Library of Congress Catalog Card Number: 60-13496

Contents

5

A Child's Garden

We have the loveliest garden,
It's called a Kindergarten.
We've variety and profusion
(Though some would say confusion!).
Variety provides the spice they say;
Our garden is new each day.

We cannot predict a bloom—
Here in their own special room,
These little ones sprout at will.
Each sign of growth brings a thrill—
This pattern is His design;
Not our plan, but His divine.

This our task, our privilege rare:
The Master Gardener's work to share.
With His guidance give our best;
Though we stumble, still find rest
In faith secure: God's great love
Directs their growth from above.*

Catherine Rogers

* Used by permission of the author.

Chapter I

The Church Plans the Weekday School for Young Children

PURPOSE

The church's weekday program for its young children falls into two age-group levels. The group provided for the three-year-olds is known as a nursery school; the group for four- and five-year-olds is called a kindergarten.

This weekday program has a "unique function in the church and community. Its responsibility goes beyond that of the public or private kindergarten. As an agency of the church it is obligated not only to offer a program consistent with the highest type of . . . [early childhood] education, but also to provide an atmosphere and program in which children and teachers are learning to live in a Christlike way. This gives the church one of its best opportunities for religious education."

In guiding the religious growth of young children as response to God in their thinking, feeling, and acting, "we must be sure that a Christian interpretation underlies all the experiences through which the child is learning. In this Christian interpretation of experience the teacher will draw from many resources, such as, suitable Bible stories and passages, worshipful moments, prayers, songs, conversation, and most of all, will count on the Christian attitudes and conduct prevalent in both the leaders and children for her teaching material.

"If properly conducted, the weekday church kindergarten has another unique function. It may be an effective means of evangelism, both by bringing parents into the church, and by helping them to establish thoroughly Christian homes."[1]

Values of Weekday Church School

Spiritually

The church-sponsored weekday nursery school and the kindergarten help the young child to grow spiritually. Under the wise guidance of teachers who know and radiate the Christian faith the child comes to know a more excellent way of life.

The living example of the teachers and the happy, Christian atmosphere which they create in the day-by-day living and maintain in the total school environment make significant impressions on the child. These nonverbal learning experiences promote the development of Christlike feelings and attitudes which find expression in the child's interpersonal relationships in school and out. In this environment the child receives a Christian interpretation of life on his level of comprehension.

"In a church-sponsored school, with Christian teachers, God will be present, acknowledged, and real. Response to the revelation of His creative power, His law, His love will be encouraged on the young child's own level. The way of love will be learned as it is lived. Children, learning through play to love their brothers whom they can see, will also begin to love God whom they cannot see."[2]

The young child who feels happy and secure in the atmosphere of the church building and with those who work in the church will develop a real sense of being a part of the Christian community who make up the church. As he associates happy times with the church, he comes to think of it very personally as his church, his friends.

Emotionally

The good weekday church nursery school and kindergarten help the young child to grow *emotionally*. He develops healthy feelings about himself—that he is a good and worthwhile person. He develops a feeling of competence and satisfaction in the mastery of new skills and in experiencing success as he experiments and works creatively with various materials. He learns through opportunities made possible in a free, permissive atmosphere to express himself—to get rid of hostility and tensions in a socially accepted manner and to feel accepted himself by his teachers and his peers. In his daily experiences he learns to accept changes and disappointments without being unduly disturbed.

As the child lives in the group, he becomes aware of his teacher's interest in and love for each individual child. Because he loves and admires her, he wants to act as she does. Through this emulation the child develops the *beginnings* of kindly feelings, consideration and concern for others, a spirit of helpfulness, tolerance, sympathy, and generosity. Through happy experiences in his group the child builds positive attitudes toward school which lay a foundation for continuing wholesome attitudes toward his educational experiences in the years to follow.

Socially

The weekday church nursery school and kindergarten help children to grow *socially*. They offer the child companionship with children of about the same developmental level and with similar interests and abilities. They offer the child companionship with teachers and other adults who share in broadening his social horizons. Good group experiences help lay the foundation for natural, wholesome social development of the young child.

Through his school experiences, both firsthand and vicarious, the child gains deeper understandings and a greater awareness and appreciation of the world around him.

As the child lives with his peers in this setting, he learns to be thoughtful of others. He learns to adjust to the group, to get the feeling of being a part of the group, and to enjoy living in a group. He grows in his ability to make worthy contributions to group activities, to develop happy friendships, and to make willingly such modifications in his behavior as the group living requires.

He begins to understand the rudiments of democratic living— of pooling his thoughts and efforts for the common good, giving and taking in good spirit, and respecting the rights, property, and accomplishments of others. He learns to share work and play materials and to take turns without frustration. He is also beginning to recognize that as a self he, too, has rights which he must learn to protect.

In many of the routine activities in the group the child begins to develop a sense of responsibility. He learns to care for his own possessions and to attend to his personal needs. He participates in clean-up activities during the school day, helping to keep the room orderly and attractive. While the child is learning to become a part of the group, he is learning at the same time to become independent, and to maintain his individuality within the group.

Mentally

Under the wise guidance of well-trained teachers in the weekday church school the child develops *mentally*. The teachers provide for the child an environment of firsthand experiences which stimulate his curiosity and imagination and contribute to his development of ideas and concepts. Many experiences the child has call for critical thinking and the solving of problems from his everyday living in the group.

Through the use of play equipment, particularly that which stimulates dramatic play, the child develops his skill in language usage. He learns to experiment widely with materials and to express his own ideas through the use of a variety of media. In the good weekday school for young children, each child is allowed to develop in his own way at his own rate of speed.

Physically

The church-sponsored weekday nursery school and kindergarten must protect the health and safety of the young child and help him to develop *physically*.

The child's large muscles are developed and he grows in motor co-ordination through the use of proper play equipment and a variety of work and play activities both indoors and out. The child is learning how to control his muscles and make them do what he wants them to do.

He learns good health habits and has opportunities to practice them daily in such routine activities as washing his hands after toileting and before eating, relaxing at regular rest times, attending to his personal needs as they arise, playing out of doors, and wearing proper clothing according to the demands of weather.

The school makes every effort possible to protect the child's health that he may grow in normal, wholesome ways which are best for him as an individual.

Values to the child's home

The weekday church nursery school and kindergarten contribute much to the homes of the children enrolled in the school.

Parents who enter into the life of their young child in his experi-

ences at the church nursery or kindergarten gain a deeper appreciation for the local church's total program of Christian education, and
thus a closer tie of home and church is formed.

As they co-operate with the teachers for the welfare of their child
and the others in the group, they find that they make progress as
parents. Through guided reading and participation in the opportunities provided for study and discussion with other parents in the
group, they come to understand themselves better and acquire knowledge of more effective ways of carrying out their parental responsibilities in the home.

As they observe their child in the school with other children, they
gain new concepts of what children are like at his stage of development. They discover something of his age-stage abilities and limitations and can therefore hold to more appropriate expectancies for the
child's behavior. They come to realize that at comparable stages of
development all youngsters have similar problems.

When parents learn to trust and have confidence in the teacher,
they will seek her counsel and guidance. As they gain new insights
into the nature of the young child and acquire new skills in guidance,
they become better equipped as Christian parents and leaders in the
church and more effective citizens of their community.

For many parents the weekday church nursery school or kindergarten is their first school contact. This association can help parents
better understand modern school practices. Good relationships for
future school experiences can be established as parents grow in
their appreciation of the values of shared experiences in their relationship with the nursery school or kindergarten staff.

Parents who may not have been vitally connected with the church
often find themselves with an awakened interest in the church as a
result of their experiences in their child's through-the-week church
school. Active participation of these parents in young adult classes
or parents' classes in the church school often grows out of such an
awakening.

The church-sponsored through-the-week school has the potential
to exert significant and far-reaching influence in the nurture of
Christian family life in the local church.

Values to the church

When the weekday church nursery school or the kindergarten is
an integral part of the total educational program of the church, it
can do much toward strengthening the work of the entire church.

Through their programs of parent education, adults are brought into a more vital relationship with the church. There are often evangelistic opportunities for reaching unchurched families who either have children in the kindergarten or have them enrolled for future attendance in the school.

Parents who study, observe, and participate in the weekday program for young children frequently become potential Sunday church school leaders for this age group.

A good nursery school or kindergarten which maintains high standards of operation stimulates improvement of the physical facilities and teaching skills in other departments of the children's division. In many churches the kindergarten director is also director of children's work. This has several advantages for the local church. There can be closer correlation between the Sunday and weekday programs for young children. The inter-staff relationships can be strengthened as tensions are relieved between the lay workers in the Sunday program and the professional people of the weekday program. As these leaders plan together for the children, mutual benefit to both programs will result.

Young adult classes often take on renewed enthusiasm when they relate themselves to some need of others which they can help meet. This might be in helping to provide scholarship funds for a child's tuition to the school. Or it might be in working with the kindergarten director on a project of repairing and making useful play equipment for the school.

As the director of the weekday program for young children interprets the purposes of the school and reports from time to time on its progress, the church membership is made more aware of the scope of the church's Christian education program for its children. And as the church effectively ministers to young children and their parents through a weekday nursery school and kindergarten, it makes more effective its Christian witness in the community of which it is a part.

Considerations Before Undertaking a Weekday Program for Young Children Under Six

When a local church has under consideration sponsoring a weekday nursery for its three-year-olds or a kindergarten for its four- or five-year-olds, it should give adequate time for study, consultation, and planning.

The official board of the local church, through its committee or commission on Christian education, should set up a *study committee*. This committee should have in its membership a representative of the official board, a person who is trained in the church's work of the children's division (director of children's work, superintendent of the children's division, or children's work counselor), a professional educator (preferably a consultant or supervisor in early childhood education), a pediatrician, and a parent of a preschool-age child. The pastor and director of Christian education should be consulting members of this group.

To explore the needs for a church-sponsored weekday nursery school or kindergarten the committee would take the following steps:

Make a survey of the families in the church to determine the needs that exist among the church constituency.

Make a survey of the needs of other families in the community who might be interested in the church's weekday program for their young children.

Counsel with the administration of the public school system.

Make a study of the number of private and church-sponsored nursery schools or kindergartens presently serving the community—their enrollments and the tuition fee charged.

The survey would need to reveal such data as:

Number and names of parents requesting the school for each of three years beyond the current year.

Number of local church families interested in having their child attend a church nursery school or kindergarten.

Number of other families in the community interested in having their child attend a church nursery or kindergarten.

Number and names of families requesting a school for three-year-olds.

Number and names of families requesting a school for four- and five-year-olds.

Number and names of families needing an all-day school.

Number and names of families preferring half-day school.

Number of parents interested in a good parent education program in connection with the school.

If no public kindergarten is offered, the number of five-year-old children available for enrollment in a church-sponsored kindergarten for each of the next three years.

If the public school kindergarten is offered, number of four-year-olds available for enrollment for a five-day kindergarten.

Number of three-year-olds available for enrollment in a two- or three-day program under the sponsorship of the church.

Reasons parents give for wanting the opportunity of a church-sponsored school for children under six.

If the results of the committee's study show a definite need for a church-sponsored school, the next step will be a study of the local church's facilities to determine whether or not the church can provide adequately for the type of weekday program needed:

State and local building codes should be thoroughly investigated. Local health and welfare departments should be consulted to ascertain whether or not the church will be able to satisfy all safety and sanitary codes for a school for young children.

Check standards for adequate indoor space and outdoor play space. (Send to State Department of Education for printed Statement of Standards and requirements, also see chapter on standards.)

All usable equipment available for the church's program should be carefully checked and an inventory made to determine the church's needs to meet the standards of a weekday school.

Check the inventory listing against the equipment recommended in chapter on standards.

When the committee's study shows there are sufficient needs to warrant the program and that the church has or can provide facilities necessary for such a program, the official board will want to make further studies with regard to finance and housing before taking official action to organize a weekday church program for young children.

After the church officials have taken the necessary action for sponsoring the weekday school for young children, they will delegate the responsibility of organizing and setting up the school to the commission, board, or committee on Christian education. Because this entire body does not have the time and is not altogether qualified for the task, it appoints and then delegates the responsibility to a kindergarten committee. This committee, since it receives its authority from the Christian education committee (board or commission), is in turn responsible to the Christian education committee.

The membership of the committee should be made up of people who are directly concerned with some phase of the school. When possible, there should be one *professional educator* serving on the kindergarten committee. The *leading teachers or superintendents of the Sunday church kindergarten and three-year-old nursery class* should be included among the membership because their classrooms and some of the children in their departments will be involved in the weekday program. A *member of the official board* having some responsibility for the finances of the church can be of real assistance in business matters of the school. *Parents* should be represented on the committee also. One or two well-qualified parents can be an asset to the committee. They will bring to the committee a parent's viewpoint. They can assist in enlisting parents' help and in interpreting the school's plans and policies to other parents. The weekday teacher will serve on this committee as an *ex officio* member. Other members serving in this same capacity with her should be those persons directly responsible for the church's program of Christian education: the pastor, church school superintendent, the chairman of the board (commission or committee) of Christian education, the director of Christian education, and the superintendent of the children's division or the children's work counselor.

To this committee, along with the director of the kindergarten, are delegated the administrative responsibilities for setting up and maintaining the school. Among their responsibilities are those of planning for the publicity and promotion of the school in the church and community; planning for the wise use of the building and grounds; making policies regarding admission ages, tuition, insurance, transportation, and health requirements; promoting good public relations; recommending staff members to the official board for elections; recommending orders for needed equipment; making up a budget and planning for the administration of the financial matters of the school; providing for a parent education program of the school; promoting co-ordinated planning, working, and evaluation of the Sunday and weekday programs for children of the church under six; and making regular reports to the board (committee or commission) of Christian education.

Budget

The cost of operating the school will be determined by the following factors:

the size of the enrollment, which determines the number of staff members
and amount of space and equipment needed;
the length of the daily sessions;
whether or not the school operates on double session;
the number of months the school is to be in session;
whether or not the director has other responsibilities in the Christian education
program, such as director of children's work.

With a background of the findings of its survey each local church
situation will determine the appropriate tuition, the need for
scholarship funds, and the size of the budget and the items covered.
The expenses of the school to be cared for in the budget will include: salaries, substitute salaries, social security, janitorial services,
equipment and expendable supplies, insurance, promotion, food,
and utilities.

The income in most church-sponsored schools will come from
tuition and the general church budget. It is next to impossible for
the school to maintain high standards and at the same time be self-
supporting by tuition alone. When the church assumes the sponsorship of the school and considers the school a part of the total
Christian education program, it should be willing to assume part
of the cost of operation of the school. The church might well under-
take, as a permanent investment, the heavy initial cost of preparing
needed facilities and providing equipment. It could also include in
the general budget such items as utilities, general maintenance and
repairs, janitorial services, social security, insurance, bookkeeping,
office supplies, and postage.

Regardless of the size of the school, there should be one person
appointed to handle the funds and keep the books. For obvious
reasons the director should not be expected to assume this responsibility.

Selection of Staff

Most important to an effective through-the-week church-sponsored
school for the young child is the teaching staff. Well-qualified leadership with training and experience in early childhood education and
Christian education is essential. Finding such leadership is difficult.
There are, however, several sources which the church may explore
in recruiting its weekday teachers.

Most colleges and universities offering programs of teacher education have some organizational setup for giving guidance to their

seniors in the matter of teacher placement. Some such schools maintain a continuing placement service for their graduates, furnishing, on request, descriptions of vacancies in the field of their specialization.

Churches which register their needs with college placement bureaus may find them to be helpful sources in locating the kind of professional leadership desired.

Some few denominations are offering in their colleges training for the church's weekday program for the young child.

While a local teacher placement bureau is a source of possible leadership, it is a little doubtful that the church would find through placement agencies teachers with specialized training in early childhood education and Christian education.

The church may find among its own college group a young woman who would like to serve in the weekday church kindergarten upon graduation. It would be better to use her as an assistant in the school than to think of her as the director, for this position requires a maturity needed for guiding adults as well as young children.

There may be in the local church a mother who is a former kindergarten or primary teacher and whose home responsibilities are such as would allow her the freedom to work half-days in the church weekday school. If she has the qualifications, the church might give her whatever help she needs in taking refresher courses to bring her training up-to-date and fit her for more responsible leadership with young children.

The church and particularly the kindergarten committee needs to be aware of the fact that both the nursery school and the kindergarten are highly specialized areas of childhood education and that a primary or elementary school teacher would need special training in these fields of education for the young child. In this regard, the church kindergarten committee will want to keep clearly in mind that teaching in the nursery school or the kindergarten is not just first grade teaching with the edges trimmed off!

The church, as it counsels with young people who are choosing church vocations, should place before young women having an interest in teaching, the challenge of the church's weekday program for children under six.

The members of the teaching staff of the church's weekday nursery school or kindergarten are responsible to the official board just as are the other professional members of the church staff. They work directly with the kindergarten committee and under the supervision of the church's committee or commission of Christian education.

Janitorial Services

The size of the school and the length of the daily session will determine the amount of janitorial services necessary. The all-day school would require one or more cooks who might also assist with some of the cleaning. The three-hour school day would require the services of a part-time maid or janitor who would give each playroom a thorough cleaning each afternoon after the children have been dismissed. If the church has two sessions each day, it should provide for cleaning of the room between the sessions and again following the dismissal of the afternoon group. Each local church situation will determine the extent of janitorial services necessary for maintaining scrupulously clean rooms.

Safety Precautions

Providing and maintaining a safe environment in the church nursery school and kindergarten is a primary concern of the teacher entrusted with the care of the youngsters in the group.

"Being alert to safety means observing and removing sources of danger such as protruding nails, unsteady ladders or boards not properly supported. It means giving close supervision to children who are playing together on high places, or to children who are using such potentially dangerous things as hammers, saws, and shovels. . . . The skillful teacher never relaxes her watchfulness."[3]

The following are further precautions which the teacher of young children should take as she plans and works for their safety at school:

Having all doors into the playroom opening outward.

Having all coat hooks in the recessed area of the children's lockers.

Arranging the room and outdoor play area in such a way that the most active areas have more space and offer the least opportunity for collision.

Eliminating glasses, paint jars, and china doll dishes, using instead polyethylene jars and dishes which are safe and durable.

Keeping a fire extinguisher easily accessible to adults but not to children.

Checking all play equipment regularly for splinters, sharp corners, and broken parts which might be dangerous.

Keeping sand, sawdust, or tanbark under all climbing apparatus in the play area.

Seeing that the kindergarten floor is never highly waxed, and that any water which is spilled on it is immediately wiped up.

Insurance

The church will want to be certain that it has provided adequately for liability insurance. It should explore the availability of special group education insurance which could be offered to the parents at a nominal fee. A number of leading insurance companies offer this type of pupil (and teacher) accident insurance through public and private schools.

Length of School Term

Insofar as it is practical, the local church should set the opening and closing dates and all holidays to run concurrently with those of the public school system in the local community.

Types of Programs

Whether or not the community provides public kindergarten, the needs of the parents of the church and community and the number of preschool children in the community will be determinants for the type of weekday program the church will want to promote for young children.

In communities where public kindergartens are not provided, the church would begin its program by providing for the five-year-old child. If, however, the community supports kindergartens in the public schools, the church could provide group experiences for the younger children, beginning with the four-year-olds if only one group can be properly maintained.

Under most circumstances the half-day program five days a week is adequate for the four's and five's. However, the demand for kindergarten education is so great in some places that the lengthy waiting lists have made it necessary for churches to operate on double sessions.

Where there is a need for group experiences for younger children and when the local church has adequate space, equipment, and trained leadership, the church may set up a program for three-year-olds also. A good nursery program can be provided for thirty three-year-olds each week under the guidance of one teacher and an assistant. They should be divided into two groups of not more than fifteen each. The three's could attend twice a week on alternating days, one group on Tuesdays and Thursdays and the other on Wednesdays and Fridays. If there are only fifteen three-year-old's enrolled, they might attend three days a week—Mondays, Wednesdays, and Fridays.

The All-Day Program

There are communities where the all-day programs are necessary to meet the needs of children of working parents in the church and community. If the church sponsors this service for parents and their young children, it will need to provide nursery care for the children from the time the parents leave for work until they return in the evening. This can mean that the school day for the young child extends from 8:30 A.M. to 3:30 P.M., but more than likely it will be an eight- or ten-hour day. Few churches, however, find they are faced with the need for such a program. Child Day-Care Centers in the community are frequently sponsored either by the industries in which the parents work or by an agency supported by the local community fund. Day-Care Centers, providing custodial care and nursery training, require the services of a nurse, nutritionist, and cooks, besides a larger teaching staff.

Other special requirements for an all-day program include a room furnished with small cots for afternoon nap time; a small room equipped to isolate and care for a child who might become ill at school; a well-equipped kitchen; dishes and silver for the noon meal; and dish carts for transporting food and dishes to and from the kitchen.

A church planning to provide an all-day child care program will want to have the guidance and counsel of the local agency issuing licenses for child care centers and day nurseries. In some communities this agency is the Department of Social Welfare; in others it may be the Department of Public Welfare or the local Health Department.

Suggested all-day time guide: 7:30 A.M.—5:30 P.M.

7:30 - 8:45   Arrival—health inspection
              Outdoor play in good weather
                          or
              Free play indoors

8:45 - 10:00	Quiet activities—story—discussion
	Music and rhythms
	Work-play time
	Clean-up time
10:00 - 11:00	Toileting
	Juice time
	Rest time
	Outdoor play
11:00 - 11:30	Clean-up and get ready for lunch
	Quiet activity before lunch
11:30 - 12:00	Lunch
12:00 - 2:30	Toileting, undressing for nap
	Sleep time
2:30 - 3:00	Dressing
	Snack time
3:00 - 4:30	Outdoor play in good weather or
	Free play indoors
4:30 - 5:30	Toileting—quiet activities before dismissal

As School Begins

Twenty-five five-year-olds are eagerly anticipating that first day when they will start to weekday church kindergarten. David Martin is representative of this group of children. He asks each morning, "Is today the day I go to kindergarten?" He cherishes a postal card he received from the kindergarten teacher, telling him that she would be looking for him at kindergarten on September 12. For the first week he will attend from 8:45 until 10:15 with twelve others who are enrolled for this year's term. (Another group of twelve children will attend from 10:45 until 12:00.)

As the days slowly come and go, awaiting the arrival of September 12, David and his mother frequently recall the happy time they spent in the kindergarten one morning in May. David had had such a good time playing house with some of the children and later hearing a story while his mother was busy filling in his registration blank and chatting with other mothers in an adjoining room.

David's mother is equally anxious for the opening of the kindergarten. She and Mr. Martin have read carefully the church's kindergarten booklet for parents which was given to them when they registered David. They are delighted to know that David will be living each day with boys and girls his own age with whom he will have many new and interesting learning experiences. David's parents are especially appreciative of the fact that Christian interpretations will permeate naturally the whole life of the kindergarten rather than just being vested in a Bible story, song, and prayer at a given time each morning.

Mrs. Martin is busy doing her part on the final preparations for David's entrance in kindergarten. She has just finished marking his sweaters, coats, and overshoes, so that David, as well as the teacher, can quickly indentify his personal belongings. She has a complete change of extra clothing, including a pair of bedroom shoes and socks, ready for David to have at school in case he spills his juice or has an accident with water.

David's teacher is also anxiously looking forward to the opening of school. She has been especially busy the last few weeks. Besides sending out cards to the children, she has visited each one in his home. She is planning to meet with the mothers one afternoon during the week just prior to the opening of school to begin work on the program of parent participation. At this meeting she will try to help the mothers to understand better their responsibilities and opportunities for contributing to the total life of the kindergarten. She will also try to help them see the wisdom of the beginning small groups with a shortened school day for both groups during the first two or three weeks. She will have ready for the mothers mimeographed copies of the first month's time schedule and the names of the children in each of the two groups. If the children's addresses and telephone numbers are included, it will be helpful to the parents in forming car pools during the first month of school.

Possible time guides for first week

Group I		Group II
8:45 - 10:15		10:30 - 12:00
8:45 - 9:25	Arrival, Work-and-Playtime	10:30 - 11:10
	Clean up	
9:25 - 9:40	Story time	11:10 - 11:25
	Music	

9:40 - 10:10   Toileting   11:25 - 11:55
                      Outdoor play

10:10 - 10:15   Rest before dismissal   11:55 - 12:00

If the children seem to need more time to adjust in the smaller groups, they will continue this program for the second week. The third week the children may be together but still have a shortened day of only two hours.

David's teacher might point out to the parents some of the distinct advantages of the small group and shortened day for young children as they begin their school experiences:

1. For the child who is experiencing for the first time separation from his mother and the security of his home, the smaller group situation assures him more individual attention from the teacher.

2. The shortened school day enables the child to adjust more easily to his new environment in that it necessitates limiting the variety of activities in which he may engage. (This also serves to guard against the danger of the child's becoming overstimulated.)

3. Having the children in small groups gives the teacher a better opportunity for getting to know each child individually and for recognizing some of his needs and abilities. Likewise, the child becomes acquainted more quickly with the teacher and his peers, and feels more at home and comfortable with them in the group.

4. In the small group it is much easier and more interesting for the child to learn such routines as caring properly for his wraps and other personal belongings, finding desired play equipment and work materials, cleaning up and putting materials away, and using the drinking fountain and toilet facilities.

David's teacher is preparing very carefully for the children's beginning school experiences. She is arranging the kindergarten room so that it is not only attractive, but stimulating for eager, curious five-year-olds. She will make easily available to the children materials and equipment which require little or no guidance or restriction in their use. She will be careful to have packed away those materials to which she does not yet want the children introduced. She has discovered that too many and varied toys and materials distract children, keeping them from having satisfying play experiences and retarding their emotional growth. David's teacher, however, will have out on the shelves some books and toys with which the children are already familiar at home and in the Sunday church kindergarten.

With all the careful planning and preparation for the beginning days, David's teacher knows that she may have a few children in the group who will find life most unhappy without the presence of their mothers. (Sometimes, however, it is apparent that it is the mother who needs help in "giving up" her child for the morning!)

In anticipating the children's reactions, David's teacher recognizes that each individual situation will need to be met in the best interest of the child involved. She realizes that occasionally it may be the point of wisdom for the mother to remain nearby, so that the child may be reassured of her presence from time to time. In no case, however, would the teacher want the mother to wait until the child is absorbed with an activity and then slip away.

David's teacher realizes, too, that sometimes a child who finds it hard to adjust will feel more secure in his strange, new environment when allowed to keep with him one of his favorite toys from home. In such a case the teacher will encourage the parent to plan with the child to bring one of his best-loved toys with him to school. The teacher will warn the parents against embarrassment if the child selects his old, tattered, one-eyed, three-legged teddy bear to give him comfort in the absence of familiar surroundings. Such a possession can be the one thing which ties him to the familiar, and even temporarily substitutes for the security he knows at home. The teacher is relatively confident that, as the child progresses in his adjustment, he will find little or no need for the "crutch," and that finally the time will come when he will discard it altogether.

With the opening of school close at hand, David's teacher and his parents are planning and working together to make the first days at kindergarten happy, satisfying experiences, for they know that these first impressions will have much bearing on his adjustment in the group and on his growth and development during the months ahead.

Building a Daily Time Guide

Because there are so many factors which must be considered in planning a daily program, it is impossible to arrive at a time schedule which would meet the needs of all young children equally well and at the same time be entirely acceptable to all nursery or kindergarten teachers. Each teacher will need to study the background, potentialities, and specific needs of the individuals of her own group and then plan for their daily experiences at school in the light of this knowledge and of the contributions which the environment and her own talents can make toward realizing the happiest, most profitable experiences for everyone.

There are, however, a few basic principles about which teachers need to be concerned as they plan for the day's program in any nursery school or kindergarten:

1. The school day should be set up in big blocks of time—in large areas of living and learning. This allows for more leisurely, unhurried movement from one activity to another.

2. The daily program of activities needs to be consistent enough to give young children a sense of security in knowing what to expect but flexible enough to encourage initiative, to permit the use of unexpected opportunities as they arise, and to adapt the length of the activity to satisfy the needs and interests of the group.

3. The times young children are expected to sit in one place should be kept short. Young children fatigue more quickly from sitting for a short time than they do in running and playing hard for a much longer period of time.

4. Juice time and the reclining rest time should come at approximately the same time each day, as they have to do with meeting the bodily needs of the children.

5. Quiet activities should always precede and follow the midmorning juice time.

6. There should be a balance and rhythm of active and quiet experiences during the day. Good activities can be practically useless and even harmful when scheduled at the wrong time. (For example, having rhythms immediately after strenuous outdoor play or a story after a lengthy time of quiet activities such as conversation or listening to music.)

7. Allowances should be made in the time schedule for a consideration of the weather—longer play time outdoors in good weather; longer periods to prepare for dismissal in cold or inclement weather.

8. The maturity of the children in the group should determine to a large degree the time allotment for group activities. Time allotments will then change somewhat during the year.

9. Allowing the children to begin whatever activity they choose as they arrive frees the teacher to meet each child informally and chat a bit with him as she observes his physical well-being. Formal "opening exercises" or "chapel services" at the beginning of each morning have little value for young children. Such a plan has a tendency to structure and set apart the children's religious experiences into this one, stipulated time of the session. There is usually no readiness for a worship experience in this type of planning. And

there is also the tendency in such a situation to over-verbalize or over-formalize the teachings.

10. While two-hour programs may be adequate for the three-year-olds, the two-hour programs for four- and five-year-old children cannot be recommended. They are too short to allow for as wide a variety of activities as these children need. They discourage the expansion of the child's interest span because of the fact that the changes in types of activities must come at too frequent intervals. However, where it is impossible to provide a longer school day, it is better to have two *unhurried* hours for the children in kindergarten than to deny them the group experiences altogether.

A suggested time guide for a three-hour kindergarten

9:00 - 10:00   Work-play time
                Clean-up activities

10:00 - 11:00   Group experiences: story time, worship, singing and rhythms
                Toileting and preparation for juice time
                Juice time
                Rest and relaxation

11:00 - 11:45   Outdoor play

11:45 - 12:00   Group experiences: science experiences, simple games, or
                   listening to music
                Preparation for dismissal (quiet time)

Each individual teacher will need to plan and experiment until she discovers a time guide and sequence of activities which best meet the needs of her particular group. She will always be aware of the fact that "a healthful, challenging physical environment, a wholesome emotional climate, warm social relationships, and rich intellectual stimulation can be utilized adequately *only* by wise planning of time."[4]

Correlation Between Weekday and Sunday Sessions

The teachers of the weekday nursery and kindergarten groups have an excellent opportunity for enriching and making more meaningful the children's Sunday church school experience. When there is a real concern for the children's growth and development, teachers of the weekday and Sunday groups can work and plan together and greatly enhance the effectiveness of their teaching.

In the departmental planning sessions there should be an exchange of information concerning the children and their church activities. This also will be the time for considering any problems relating to space or the use and storage of equipment.

The weekday teachers should co-operate in leaving the kindergarten rooms on Friday ready for the preparation the church school teacher will make before the Sunday session. The same is true of the Sunday church teachers as they leave the rooms after the Sunday session. Both groups will find it simpler if they can have separate storage cabinets for their expendable materials such as crayons, paper, paste, and paints. Then the teachers in each group will know what work materials they have on hand and where they are. Of course, the large equipment such as home center and blocks should be available as needed. *Storage space should be provided for all equipment which is a part of the weekday program only.*

Interpersonal relationships are so very important for the effectiveness of both programs. The director of the weekday program will seize every opportunity for creating and maintaining harmonious relations between the teachers of the Sunday church school and those of the weekday groups. She will, with the help of the kindergarten committee, promote in the church the understanding that the weekday program for young children is an integral part of the total Christian education program of the church. The children who are fortunate enough to have the opportunity of belonging to both the weekday and Sunday church kindergarten groups will have many enriching experiences as a result of the correlation in the planning of their program of activities.

The weekday teachers need to exercise great care at all times that they do not "take the edge off" the church school materials for the children by excessive usage or by inappropriate timing of their use with the weekday group. Careful planning with the Sunday church teaching staff will help to eliminate both of these difficulties.

If the weekday teachers make it a habit to know what stories, songs, and other materials have been introduced to the children in the Sunday situation, they can re-use the material and build on the children's experiences in such ways as seem needed and as the more leisurely program permits.

Interpreting the School to the Church and Community

Interpreting to the church and community the purpose of the church-sponsored, through-the-week nursery and kindergarten schools is a process which is carried on continuously through a variety of means.

The printed word rightly used can be one of the most effective media of promotion and interpretation. Most churches having a through-the-week school prepare an attractive brochure which states the purposes, philosophy, and policies of the school. This can be made available to adult classes in the church as well as to parents of young children in the community.

From time to time the church bulletin or church newsletter can be used as a channel to keep the membership informed about the school and the interesting experiences the children have. Occasionally, the values of certain types of activities might be pointed out.

Nursery school or kindergarten newsletters which are sent periodically to the parents of the children in the school would be of interest to the members of young adult classes in the local church. A file of all the newsletters sent out during the school year might well accompany the director's annual report to the official body of the church. This will add the human interest element to her reports.

Another means for interesting and informing people about the weekday program for young children is through letters from the group to individuals or members of adult classes who have had some contact with the school. These might be "thank you" letters for new equipment or for services rendered. Or they might be invitations to a parents' meeting or open house in the kindergarten. Letters will be more appealing to adults if they are dictated by the children and accompanied by several of the children's paintings. When the director wants to point out certain values, she just adds a postscript from "teacher." Incidentally, this is a subtle way of promoting a little informal parent education.

The local newspaper is another source which the church will find useful in interpreting to the community its through-the-week program for young children. Short feature stories, notices of parents' meetings, and registration announcements help to keep the public aware of the church's educational program for the young children of the community.

The director will make use of the printed word by writing interesting reports of the school and its activities for the kindergarten committee and the committee or commission on Christian education. Among other things in these reports she can point to evidences of how the purposes of the school are being realized.

The director will make use of visual materials also as she works to promote and interpret to adults the nursery-kindergarten weekday program. A bulletin board displaying pictures of the children at work and play will help to create more interest and concern for the young children in the church. The bulletin board should be exhibited in a place where most of the adults will have an opportunity to see it. Color slides taken of the children showing typical experiences at school can be used effectively at a family night meeting at the church. A well-planned script to accompany the slides will convey to the adults of the church something of what is meant by a good weekday church kindergarten program for the young child.

When the director participates in civic and professional groups in the community, she will have occasion from time to time to speak to individuals and perhaps to the group about the church's educational provision for young children in the weekday program. With these opportunities comes the responsibility for building good public relations.

Along during the year several members of the Christian education committee or commission, members of the official board, and other key people in the church should be invited to have some firsthand experience with the school. It might be that several would be invited to enjoy the work-playtime with the group some morning. At another time some of the church friends might be invited to accompany the group on an excursion. Such experiences will make for staunch supporters of the school. When the key people in the church's program of Christian education are informed and enthusiastic about the school, they in turn will help greatly in building good relationships with the school and a better understanding of its purposes and values for young children.

Having an Open House in the kindergarten sometime in the spring will pay rich dividends in helping the church become more concerned about the kindergarten program. The room should be set up according to interest centers with the work and play materials in readiness for activity. Children's art work—their paintings and clay and woodwork creations—should be on display with explanatory labels. Snapshots of the children at work and play might be exhibited with brief explanatory notes. Parents can add to the effectiveness of the Open House by helping to explain about the various aspects of the program. This will call for more detailed planning with the parents, but it will also mean that more people will hear more about the school than would be possible with only the weekday church school staff as hostesses.

As the director meets with the parents of the children enrolled in the weekday program, the kindergarten committee, the church's committee on Christian education, the workers' conferences, and children's division council, she will have many occasions to interpret by the spoken word the philosophy, purposes, and curriculum for the nursery-kindergarten weekday program.

Well-informed parents do an excellent job of promoting the school and helping other parents to get a "parent's-eye view" of the church's program for its young children.

Young children should *never be used* to promote the school or interpret what it teaches! "Programs" in which the children perform (particularly at Christmas and the closing of school to show what they have learned and how good the teachers are) are definitely harmful to the children. In every way possible the church will guard against exploiting the young child in its care.

This does not mean, however, that the children will not help to interpret phases of the school program to their parents and neighbors. Their growth and development and their "learnings" at the weekday church school are "proof of the pudding." These learnings show up incidentally in the young children's relationships in their home and neighborhood. Children "tell" much of what they learn through their growing independence and maturity as a result of the good group experiences they have had in nursery school or kindergarten.

Chapter II

Standards for Good Nursery-Kindergarten Education

Ages to Be Accepted

Churches able to provide adequately for only one age group would begin with the five-year-old group, unless, of course, the local community provides for the kindergarten program in the public schools. In this event, the church might want to provide for the four-year-olds. If space, equipment, and good leadership permit, a program for three-year-old children could be provided. The church will be guided in its weekday offerings by the needs of the families of its constituency and of others in the community.

Size of Groups

Limiting the number of children enrolled according to the age group is essential for the best development of the children. The five-year-old group should be limited to twenty-five, while the four-year-old group should not exceed twenty. The three-year-olds will have the best experiences if there are no more than fifteen in a group. One teacher and one assistant are needed for each group of children.

Qualifications of Teachers

"The educational standard for a qualified teacher in a nursery school or kindergarten in the church should be at least equivalent to the public school standard on the early childhood level in the community, plus a knowledge of the principles of Christian growth for young children."[1]

This would mean that the director would have a bachelor's degree from an accredited college. She should have twelve semester hours in nursery-kindergarten training, four semester hours in child development, and fifteen semester hours in religious education.

The assistant teacher, who does not have the responsibility of

33

teaching without supervision, should have at least two years of college, including eight semester hours in early childhood education and three semester hours in child development. She could be expected to further her education in an in-service training program under the guidance of the kindergarten director.

The following description of what it means to be called "My Teacher" by a young child sets forth the qualifications which a teacher of young children should possess.

It means:

1. *To accept other people warmly.*

"My teacher" understands children's feelings. She acknowledges children's sorrows, angers, hurts, and fears. She lets them know that she, too, experiences these same feelings. She sympathizes rather than censures. She helps each child to feel wanted and important.

Young children are spontaneous. "My teacher" shares their fun, joy, and excitement. She does not rely on false dignity to impress others.

"My teacher" is at ease with people. She is a friend of children and adults. She can forget her teacher-role sufficiently to let herself be taught.

2. *To appreciate children for what they are.*

"My teacher's" genuine liking for young children will make for patience in dealing with them. She recognizes them as personalities who are learning. Children at five are still struggling to master many skills and ideas. As a result, they are often painfully slow and awkward in such simple things as dressing, responding to instructions, or putting away toys. They are "awkward" in social relations, also.

The teacher is able to stimulate and encourage the child's interest in self expression. She is appreciative of each child's effort and understanding enough to be able to give him the time and encouragement he needs to improve and to grow in independence.

3. *To understand individual differences in children.*

"My teacher" looks for the cause of various types of behavior. She understands that only as she removes the causes of undesirable behavior will that child's behavior improve.

Children entering kindergarten show a wide range of maturity—physically, mentally, socially, and emotionally. If a teacher attempts to "treat them all alike," she can only frustrate herself and the children. "My teacher" studies the needs of each child, and responds to each in terms of his needs.

4. *To be a good leader.*

"My teacher" wins the respect of the group by being fair, firm, and explicit. In general, they [the children] are eager to cooperate if they understand what is expected of them. A loved and respected teacher will inspire true cooperation from children and adults.

5. *To feel personal security.*

"My teacher" has a sense of well being. She respects her own part in the building of a desirable society. She wins appreciation from groups and is loved by individuals. To be competent to handle the fears, emotional problems, and special needs of young children, a teacher needs self-confidence, and a knowledge that she is respected in the community.

6. *To possess emotional stability.*

"My teacher" has a happy, wholesome outlook on life. She thoroughly enjoys living. Without losing sight of the final goal she is satisfied to take the moment —the hour—each day as it comes and make the most of it!

The effective teacher has a sense of balance and a sense of humor. She finds help in the quotation, "Give me the strength to endure those things which can not be changed, the courage to change those things which can be changed, and the wisdom to know the difference between the two." Her best remedy for certain problems, however, is to be able to laugh at them and then forget them if they do not justify or permit remedy by direct attack.

7. *To possess a margin of reserve energy and poise.*

"My teacher" has vitality and endurance. She can come through a strenuous day with a smile and waken the next morning eager for the privileges and responsibilities which that day brings.

8. *To have broad interests.*

"My teacher" feels real enthusiasm and curiosity for the world outside the classroom. She is interested in experimenting with materials, in investigating the community, and in the whole business of living. She, too, is a learner, and often a learner with children. She appreciates the good, the true, and the beautiful wherever she finds these qualities.

9. *To feel a dedication to her work.*

"My teacher" has a professional attitude. She enjoys her work and believes in it. She thinks about her work, asks herself questions, and tries to answer these through observation and study. She sees needs and is resourceful in trying to meet them. Her easy relaxed manner which produces an inner calm among those with whom she associates does not mean she is "easy going." Her skill, anticipation of needs, and thoughtful preparation make her task appear easy but they result from sincere effort. She is both subjective and objective in her work. She is becoming a better person as she becomes a better teacher. "My teacher" uses both her head and her heart![2]

10. *To be a growing person.*

"My teacher" reads and studies in order that she may understand young children better and improve her ways of guiding them. She also attends professional meetings in her community.

11. *To be a sincere Christian.*

"My teacher" is a sincere Christian friend. She has an intelligent and positive Christian faith which is evidenced in her day-by-day living with the children and other adults.

12. *To be concerned with the children's religious growth.*

"My teacher" understands religion on the young child's level. She seeks to discover the religious needs of individuals in the group and tries to meet those needs in ways which the young child can understand. She will not introduce religious concepts which are beyond his ability to perceive. She knows that play for the young child is an important way of learning for him, so she will give him many opportunities each day for learning how to live and get along with his peers and his teachers in a Christian way. She realizes that much of his religious learning results from the nonverbal method. And she knows that worship for the nursery- and kindergarten-age child may come in fleeting moments, so she must be aware of his responses to God in situations and be sensitive to times when individuals as well as the group show a readiness to worship.

Duties of the Staff

In a large, church-sponsored nursery-kindergarten the director would have the supervision of the teachers, guide the program for children and parents, hold staff meetings, be responsible for the program of parent education, keep all records, make reports to the church's kindergarten committee, attend nursery and kindergarten departmental planning sessions and church school workers' conferences, and plan with the leading teacher or superintendent of the Sunday church kindergarten for correlation of activities.

In a small school the director would also be responsible for one group of children. In churches where provision is made for only one group, the director is often employed by the church to direct the work of the children's division of the church as well as the weekday kindergarten. This combination of duties makes it possible for the church to provide a salary which is attractive to a well-qualified teacher. It means also that the effectiveness of the educational program for the children of the church will be greatly strengthened. However, when there is a combination of responsibilities, the church should be careful in the job analysis to make certain that the teacher has the time needed for all the kindergarten responsibilities which require her time *beyond* the daily morning session.

The responsibilities of the teacher of each group would be planning the curriculum, keeping individual records on children, having conferences with parents of children in the group, attending parents' meetings, attending staff meetings and kindergarten departmental meetings, and making reports to the official board as requested.

In-Service Training

Most public school systems require their teachers to take additional college courses periodically, that they may continue growing in the profession. Some systems have set up area teacher education extension services in co-operation with colleges and universities. These courses are offered in the school community in the afternoons or on Saturdays on alternating weeks throughout the school year. This makes it possible for teachers to receive additional training without the added expenses of summer school. Some teachers' colleges offer Saturday morning classes for teachers on their campuses.

The church kindergarten committee should explore all the local opportunities offered for in-service training which would help the church kindergarten staff to keep growing in professional effectiveness.

There are a number of informal in-service training opportunities which the church-sponsored weekday nursery school or kindergarden can make available as a means of helping the members of its staff grow in understanding and skills in their teaching responsibilities:

providing professional books, pamphlets, and periodicals for teachers' reading and study;

maintaining an effective program of parent education;

having well-planned, purposeful staff and kindergarten committee discussion meetings;

encouraging membership and participation in local professional associations for teachers of young children.

Affiliations

It is of great importance that every effort be made for establishing and maintaining good relations between the weekday church school, the public school administration, and other nursery schools and kindergartens operating within the community.

For her professional growth the teacher will want to become an active member of local professional groups for teachers of early childhood education.

The following are professional organizations through which teachers of young children find much practical help:

A. C. E. I.

Many communities have a local branch of the Association for Childhood Education International, which is a professional organization extending membership to any person interested in the welfare of children. If there is no branch in the community, and if there are those who desire the professional benefits of the Association, they may join through the national office and receive the magazine *Childhood Education* as well as a number of the Association's helpful publications each year. Or they may consider organizing a local branch of the Association. In either case, communications should be sent to: Association for Childhood Education International, 3615 Wisconsin Avenue, N. W., Washington 16, D. C.

SACUS

The Southern Association on Children Under Six is a nonprofit, self-supporting organization composed of persons in the thirteen Southern states who are working with or interested in the welfare of preschool-age children. The state groups hold regional or state workshops and conferences annually. Further information may be obtained by writing to: SACUS, Berea College, Berea, Kentucky.

NANE

NANE stands for the National Association for Nursery Education. This organization fosters the advancement of good education for young children ready for group experience. It publishes a quarterly journal, holds a national conference biennially, and produces a reliable source of inexpensive materials interpreting nursery education. For further information about the Association and its publications write to: NANE, 155 East Ohio Street, Room 200, Chicago 11, Illinois.

Salary and Teacher Benefits

The salary of the director and teachers in the church-sponsored nursery school and kindergarten should be determined by each teacher's professional education, teaching experience, and responsibilities, and should be comparable to the remuneration received by the local public school teachers having similar professional training and experience.

Teacher benefits should be as attractive as those offered to public school teachers. They would include Social Security, group health and accident insurance, retirement, sick leave, vacation, opportunities for various types of in-service training, and salary increments dependent upon the fulfillment of stipulated requirements.

Nursery School and Kindergarten Facilities

Indoor Space

The rooms used for nursery and kindergarten through-the-week programs should be located on the ground floor of a fireproof building. Southern and eastern exposure is preferable.

The rooms should provide for from 35 to 45 square feet per child for a group of twenty-five five-year-olds, twenty four-year-olds, or fifteen three-year-olds.

The bathroom should be directly accessible to the playroom and convenient to the outdoor play area. It should provide one toilet and one lavatory for each eight children enrolled. These should be scaled to child size. Toilet seats should be 10 inches high for nursery and kindergarten children. Low partitions (without doors) should separate the compartments. "Doors present hazards for fingers and interfere with the casual matter-of-factness of the situation as well as with the ease of supervision."[3] The hand lavatories should be 23 inches high and should provide warm and cold water. The plumbing in the lavatories should be regulated so that the child has to wash his hands under the running water. This is essential for proper sanitation and it will also insure against a flooded bathroom from an overflowing lavatory.

A coatroom near the outdoor entrance and adjacent to the play area should contain individual, open lockers marked with identifying pictures selected by each child. The lockers should provide a compartment for hats, gloves, and other small personal belongings; a lower compartment with hooks for wraps; and a lower section for galoshes and rubbers.

Provision should be made for the proper care of the teachers' wraps and personal belongings.

There should be some room or space outside the playroom for isolation in case of illness.

Adequate storage space makes for good school housekeeping. Open shelves which can be adjusted to the types of work and play equipment need to be low so they will be accessible to the children. When the tops of the open shelves are no higher than 24 inches, they may be used for work activities and for displaying books, science materials, growing plants, puzzles, and other small equipment. This arrangement is an excellent space-saver. Closed storage space is also essential for work material and equipment which is not available for the group at all times.

Floors of Playrooms

The floors should be warm, light in color, and of a material which is easily cleaned. Asphalt tile of a good quality is practical.

Walls and Ceiling

Walls should be in light-colored, pleasing pastel tints, and of a nonglossy finish. The ceiling should be light in color and acoustically-treated. The effect of noise and color on the "emotional tone" of the playroom can hardly be overemphasized.

Ventilation and Heating

The health and comfort of the group are greatly dependent upon proper heating and ventilation of the rooms. The heating-ventilating system should be able to maintain room temperatures between 68° and 72° at the level of the children's height. The heat should be diffused evenly over the room without causing drafts. Where manual ventilation is necessary, window deflectors should be installed to avoid direct currents of cold air blowing on the children. If radiators are a part of the heating system, they should be covered in a way that will protect the children from bumping into them or being burned.

Lighting

Lighting in all areas of the playroom should measure 20-40 footcandle light. The light should be well diffused and so controlled as to eliminate all glare.

Windows which have eastern and southern exposures are preferable. They should be low enough for the children to see out of them, no higher than 24 inches from the floor. Adequate window space for the playroom should measure at least one-fifth of the floor space of the room.

Plumbing Facilities

One projection-type drinking fountain, preferably one which is recessed in the wall, is essential for each playroom.

A sink with work counter on either side, 24 inches from the floor, plays an important part in the art and water play activities and in helping the children take the responsibility for cleaning up and for being independent about it.

For all-day nursery and kindergarten programs a kitchen near the playroom is essential.

The half-day session requires the use of kitchen facilities for refrigeration of juice, and sink for washing pitchers, trays, and storage jars, but does not necessitate the set-up of equipment required by the all-day program.

Outdoor Play Area

The outdoor play areas have as important function in the education of young children as the indoor playrooms. In fact, if the outdoor area opens directly off of the indoor classroom, it can be just an extension of the indoor area. Many of the activities of the session can be carried on equally well in either area, weather permitting.

The outdoor play area should provide for 150 to 200 square feet per child. This yard should be fenced-in to protect the children and to set boundaries for their play. The area should be well-drained and should have a balance of sunshine and shade. Part of the area should be paved for play with wheel toys. Local authorities should be consulted about the most resilient and least abrasive hard-surfacing available. Any structured play equipment should be out of the line of play.

The area should provide for quiet and active play. It should have a small plot set apart for digging. Sometimes the digging will result in a small flower or vegetable garden. Every effort possible should be made to promote the health and ensure the safety of the children in their work and play indoors and out.

Locked storage space is essential for the outdoor equipment such as wheel toys, tools, workbench, sand toys, and all portable outdoor equipment. If there is a covered terrace, the storage unit might be located at one end with a ramp for easy moving of equipment.

Provision of Library for Staff and Parents

One very effective type of informal in-service training for weekday church nursery and kindergarten teachers is a guided reading program of professional books, pamphlets, and periodicals. Teachers will want to build their own personal libraries, but churches should provide a professional library for its staff and parents.

Most chapters of this text carry a bibliography of outstanding current books and pamphlets relative to the subject discussed in the chapter. For a church planning to establish a library for its kindergarten staff and parents of young children, the following bibliography is suggested as a well-balanced, basic library, costing approximately $75.00. Those books marked (*) should be among the first purchases for the library.

Understanding Young Children

Havighurst, Robert J., *Developmental Tasks and Education*. New York: Longmans, Green & Co., 1952.
* Hymes, James L., Jr., *Understanding Your Child*. New York: Prentice-Hall, Inc., 1952.
Hymes, James L., Jr., *A Child Development Point of View*. New York: Prentice-Hall, Inc., 1955.
*New York State Education Department, *Child Development Guides for Teachers of Three-, Four-, and Five-Year-Old Children*. Albany, N. Y.: New York State Education Department, 1956.
*U. S. Department of Health, Education, and Welfare, *Your Child from One to Six*. Children's Bureau Publication, Bulletin No. 30, revised, 1956.

Developing the Program and Guidance

Barnouw, Elsa and Swan, Arthur, *Adventures with Children in Nursery School and Kindergarten*. New York: Thomas Y. Crowell Company, 1959.
Baruch, Dorothy, *New Ways of Discipline*. New York: McGraw-Hill Book Co., 1949.
Baruch, Dorothy, *Understanding Young Children*. New York: Teacher's College, Columbia University, 1949.
Campbell, Elizabeth W., *Security for Young Children*. Boston: Pilgrim Press, 1952.
Chittenden, Gertrude, *et al., Essentials of Nursery Education*. National Association for Nursery Education, Distribution Center, University of Rhode Island, Kingston, R. I.
* Denominational Curriculum Materials.
Dept. of Kindergarten-Primary Education, *Foundation Learnings in the Kindergarten*. National Educational Association. 1201 16th St., N.W., Washington 6, D. C.
Dook, Elizabeth, *What Does the Nursery School Teacher Teach?* National Association for Nursery Education, Distribution Center, University of Rhode Island, Kingston, R. I.
* Fairly, John L. and Arleene, *Using the Bible to Answer Questions Children Ask*. Richmond, Va.: John Knox Press, 1958.
Fletcher, Margaret, *The Adult and the Nursery School Child*. Toronto, Canada: University of Toronto Press, 1958.

*Fritz, Dorothy B., *The Spiritual Growth of Children*. Philadelphia: The West-minster Press, 1957.

*Gaitskell, Charles and Margaret, *Art Education in the Kindergarten*. Peoria, Ill.: Chas. A. Bennett Co., Inc., 1952.

Gans, Roma, Stendler, Celia, *et al., Teaching Young Children*. New York: World Book Co., 1952.

Gesell, Arnold and Ilg, Frances, *Infant and Child in the Culture of Today*. New York: Harper & Brothers, 1943.

Green, Marjorie M. and Woods, Elizabeth, *A Nursery School Handbook for Teachers and Parents*. Sierra Madre, California: Sierra Madre Community Nursery School, 1954.

* Hartley, Ruth, Frank, Lawrence K., *et. al., Understanding Children's Play*. New York: Columbia University Press, 1952.

*Heffernan, Helen, Ed., *Guiding the Young Child*. Boston: D. C. Heath Co., 1959.

*Heinz, Mamie, *Growing and Learning in the Kindergarten*. Richmond, Va.: John Knox Press, 1959.

Hymes, James L., Jr., *Behavior and Misbehavior*. New York: Prentice-Hall, Inc., 1955.

Hymes, James L., Jr., *Effective Home-School Relations*. New York: Prentice-Hall, Inc., 1953.

* Hymes, James L., Jr., *Before the Child Reads*. Evanston, Ill.: Row, Peterson & Company, 1958.

Hurlock, Elizabeth B., *Child Growth and Development*. New York: McGraw-Hill Book Co., 1956.

Jones, Mary Alice, *Guiding Children in Christian Growth*. New York: Abingdon Press, 1949.

Lambert, Hazel, *Teaching the Kindergarten Child*. New York: Harcourt, Brace & Co., 1958.

Landreth, Catherine, *Education of the Young Child*. New York: John Wiley & Sons, Inc., 1952, 1955.

* Leavitt, Jerome, Ed., *Nursery-Kindergarten Education*. New York: McGraw-Hill Book Co., 1958.

Leonard, Edith M., Vandeman, Dorothy D., *et al., Counseling with Parents in Early Childhood Education*. New York: The Macmillan Company, 1954.

Moore, Sallie B. and Richards, Phyllis, *Teaching in the Nursery School*. New York: Harper & Brothers, 1959.

(See chapter, "Working with Parents" for bibliography of pamphlets and periodicals for use with parents.)

*Read, Katherine, *The Nursery School*. Philadelphia: W. B. Saunders Co., 1955.

Redl, Fritz, *Understanding Children's Behavior*. New York: Teacher's College, Columbia University, 1957.

* Roorbach, Rosemary K., *Religion in the Kindergarten*. New York: Harper & Brothers, 1949.

Rudolph, Marguerita, *Living and Learning in Nursery School*. New York: Harper & Brothers, 1954.

Sheehy, Emma D., *The Fives and Sixes Go to School*. New York: Henry Holt & Co., Inc., 1954.

* Sheehy, Emma D., *There's Music in Children*. New York: Henry Holt & Co., Inc., 1952.

Sherer, Lorraine, *How Good Is Our Kindergarten?* Guidelines for Education of Five-Year-Olds. A. C. E. I., 3615 Wisconsin Ave., N.W., Washington 16, D.C., 1959.

*Shields, Elizabeth McE. and Mallard, Dorothae, *Guiding Kindergarten Children in the Church School*. Richmond, Va.: John Knox Press, 1931, revised 1955.

State Department of Education, *Teachers Guide to Education in Early Childhood*. Sacramento, California: State Department of Education, 1956.

Stendler, Celia and Martin, William, *Intergroup Education in Kindergarten-Primary Grades*. New York: The Macmillan Company, 1953.
Stephens, A. D., *Providing Developmental Experiences for Young Children*. New York: Teacher's College, Columbia University, 1952.
Strang, Ruth, *A Study of Young Children*. New York: Abingdon Press, 1944.
Taylor, Katharine W., *Parent Cooperative Nursery Schools*. New York: Teacher's College, Columbia University, 1954.
What Are Kindergartens For? Association for Childhood Education International, 1959.
*Ward, Muriel, *Young Minds Need Something to Grow On*. New York: Row, Peterson & Company, 1957.
Wills, Clarice and Stegeman, William, *Living in the Kindergarten*. Chicago: Follet Publishing Company, revised 1956.
Young, Lois, *Teaching Kindergarten Children*. Philadelphia: Judson Press, 1959.

Equipment and Furnishings

Chairs for the nursery group should be 8 and 10 inches high; for the kindergarten group they should be 10 and 12 inches high. Chairs for the teacher should be no higher than 14 inches.

Stacking chairs are space savers and make for better posture as there are no rungs over which the children can hook their heels. Silencers on table and chair legs add to the good emotional tone of the room.

The tables should be finished in nonglossy straw or blonde color. The finish should be stain-proof and one that is easily cleaned. They may be rectangular or trapezoidal in shape. The trapezoidal tables have the advantage of stacking to give more floor space. They may also be placed together to form different shapes for different activities. The tables need to be 10 inches higher than the chair seats.

Open Shelves

Open shelves running along one side of the wall provide storage space for small toys, books, and large blocks. If the shelves are no higher than 24 inches from the floor, the counter top may be used for the science and book centers.

Rug

Each playroom should be equipped with a rug which will accommodate all the children in the group at the same time. A good size is 12' x 15'. The color should be a neutral shade which blends in with the rest of the floor. Durable rugs are now being made of new fabrics which give the appearance of wool but are stain-resistant and are easily cleaned. The price is somewhat less than that of woolen rugs.

Tackboards

Tackboards or corkboards should be of the same color or a bit darker shade of the color of the room. They should be low enough for the children to enjoy at eye level the pictures exhibited on them. The low partition screens which are often used as room dividers in the playhouse area may be used as tack-boards. These can be moved about the room wherever special displaying of pictures is necessary—oftentimes in the discussion group area.

Chalkboards in the kindergarten are not absolutely essential. However, if wall space permits, two colored boards 21 inches from the floor and 36" x 48" in size can be useful. Children enjoy drawing with large, one-inch sticks of colored chalk on the chalkboard.

Block Bins

For the smaller unit blocks, shelf storage is unsatisfactory. A bin or large clothesbasket serves well for the storage of these blocks. These should be not more than 18" to 20" deep.

Resting Equipment

For the all-day nursery or kindergarten, provision must be made for the children's comfort in resting. Folding or stacking cots are the most satisfactory when children have long rest or nap times. For the half-day session, resting mats serve quite well. The use of rag rugs or large towels does not meet health standards as it is almost impossible to keep them sanitary. Mats which are covered with plastic can be cleaned daily. When two colors of plastic are used, one side (perhaps the darker color) can always be placed on the floor. If these can fold into three sections, they will store more easily. A good size for the resting mat is 18" x 48". This would make three equal sections of 16". Each child can furnish his own thin cotton blanket which can be folded into the mat after resting time.

Easels

Two double easels are adequate for a group of twenty-five. They should be adjustable and should have paint racks for holding the paint containers.

Folding Clothes-Drying Rack

A four-foot folding clothes rack makes an excellent place for drying the children's paintings. It is a space-saver and encourages the children to care for their own paintings without adult help.

Piano

A small piano, kept in tune, is an asset to any kindergarten.

Record Player

If there is no piano in the kindergarten, a record player is a must. With the wealth of excellent children's recordings of music and stories now available, one could almost say that the record player is on the *essential list* of equipment for kindergarten and nursery schools.

Block Center

Unit blocks of a variety of shapes and sizes should be provided in quantity —triangular, rectangular, spherical, cubical, cylindrical, elliptical curve, half-circle arch, x-switch, y-switch, and other shapes. A set of 500 unit blocks is adequate for a nursery or kindergarten when there are also large blocks for building indoors. The following are accessories for unit block play: small boards, wooden animals and people, trucks, airplanes, small boats, tractors, cars, and a small fire engine.

Where indoor space permits, large hollow blocks should be provided. These come in sizes 5½″ x 5½″ x 11″, 5½″ x 11″ x 11″, and 5½″ x 11″ x 22″. The following are accessories to the hollow block play: large boards, ramps 5½″ x 22″, fences 5½″ x 11″ x 22″, benches 5½″ x 11″ x 22″, steering wheel mounted in large block, automobile tire pump, oil cans, rubber hose, and large wooden trucks.

Home Center

This center offers opportunity for dramatic play of family life. The furniture should be scaled to child size, durable, functional, and attractive. The essentials for this center include:

kitchen stove
cooking utensils
hutch cabinet
polyethylene dishes
sink
refrigerator
small table and two chairs
doll bed (strong enough to hold kindergarten child)
doll carriage

rocking chair
chest of drawers and mirror
2 telephones
4 dolls, various sizes
box of dress-up clothes
small broom, mop, dustpan
ironing board and play iron
2 or 3 divider screens, approximately 32″ x 48″

Housekeeping Equipment

wastepaper baskets, preferably polyethylene—lightweight, soundproof, rustproof
vases and flower containers, papiermâché—lightweight, unbreakable
cellulose sponges—several sizes
dustpan—long-handled

mop and mop pail
broom
dry mop
dustcloths
toilet brush
vacuum cleaner

Kitchen Equipment

pitcher
trays
can opener
plastic breadbaskets
saucepans

cookie sheets
egg beater
tablespoons
paper cups (5 oz.)
paper towels and toilet tissue

Music Center

Refer to section on Experiencing Music Together.

Science Center
Refer to section on Experiencing Science.

Book Center
Refer to section on Experiencing Literature with Young Children.

Beauty Center

picture frame or easel for large kindergarten pictures
low vases for different kinds of flowers

large Bible
large simplified world globe

Art Materials
Refer to section on Creative Activities.

Water Play Materials
A large, flat container for floating objects and other water play is needed A small polyethylene bucket and rubber tubing are needed for siphoning water. An egg beater, a tea strainer, cellulose sponges, a small unbreakable pitcher, funnels, two-inch paint brushes, a small colander, and boats all add to the child's fun as he plays and experiments with water.

Old shower curtains, discarded plastic window curtains, and plastic tablecloths may be cut into "waterproofing" garments for the children to slip on over their clothes.

Bubble-blowing is a water play activity necessitating only the simplest of equipment: discarded cottage cheese cartons or small paper milk cartons, soapsuds, and drinking straws.

Miscellaneous Toys

For dramatic play

cash register
doctor's kit
2″ flat paintbrushes
small buckets
discarded adult clothes and accessories

For individual or small group play

wooden inlay puzzles
large wooden dominoes (for older fives)
stuffed animals
kaleidoscope
stereoscope and pictures
picture dominoes

First-Aid Kit
Minimum requirements for a first-aid kit for use in nursery and kindergarten are:

sterile gauze, 2″ and 3″ squares (small individual packets best)
bandage, 1″ and 2″

disinfectant (to be recommended by local physician)
applicators and tongue depressors

needle for removal of splinters
adhesive tape and Band-Aids
clinical thermometer (oral)
tube of white vaseline
burn ointment (to be recommended
  by local physician)
bicarbonate of soda for insect stings

scissors
splints
soap
alcohol
cotton
tweezers

Office Supplies

Fire Extinguisher

Clock

Picture File of Teaching Pictures

Outdoor Equipment

climbing apparatus—"climb-around,"
  3-way ladders
sawhorses—varying sizes from 1′ to
  4′ high, preferably 2 of each height
walking planks—10″ wide, 5′ to 6′
  long, with cleats on each end to
  secure to rungs of sawhorses
4′ and 5′ ladders
large wooden barrels and kegs—free
  from splinters
wooden boxes and crates—varying
  sizes, free from splinters and sharp
  edges
wheel toys—tricycles (different sizes),

wheelbarrows, wagons, Irish Mail
miscellaneous play materials—2 10″
  playground balls, 2 12″ playground
  balls, 4 8″ x 8″ beanbags, 4 wooden
  hoops 23″ in diameter, 2 reins, jump
  ropes, workbench, tools, scrap
  lumber
outdoor sandbox and sand toys—
  spoons, scoops, rubber shovels,
  small cars and boats, polyethylene
  colander, small plastic bucket, funnels, muffin tins, Jello molds,
  wooden spoons, sprinkler

Criteria for the Selection of Equipment and Materials

1. Is it appropriate for the age for which it is produced?
2. Is it scaled to correct size for the age children for which it is produced?
3. Does it have pleasing color, nonpoisonous paint?
4. Is it safe—no sharp edges or corners?
5. Is it attractive?
6. Can the article be used in more than one way and by more than one child?
7. Does it provide for large-muscle activity?
8. Is the article sturdy and durable?
9. Will it withstand regular cleaning and is it easily cleaned?
10. Is the price comparable to similar articles produced by other manufacturers?
11. Does the article promote growth in independence, group activity, and
    social behavior?

12. Does the article help in the development of co-ordination and muscular skills?
13. Does the article stimulate the child's curiosity, interest, and initiative?
14. Does the article help to extend the child's imagination and his creative powers?
15. Does the article provide opportunities for problem-solving and the necessity for resourcefulness on the part of the child?

Guiding Principles in Wise Selection of Equipment and Materials

1. The available budget should always be considered in the purchasing of equipment, giving priority to the essential needs.
2. Scrap materials and some well-constructed homemade equipment should be included in all kindergarten planning.
3. A wide variety of equipment is essential to meet the varying needs within the group. (Instead of five tricycles, why not two tricycles, one wagon, one large wheelbarrow, and one Irish Mail for a kindergarten group?)
4. The selection of equipment should provide for a balance of quiet and active play indoors and out.
5. The health and safety of the children should be of primary consideration in the selection of play equipment for the group.

Homemade Equipment

Homemade equipment, if well-constructed, can save decidedly on the budget. When parents can help in creating some of the equipment, they become more interested in the school's program. They often discover ways of providing simple equipment for their child in the home.

Some of the things which can be easily made for the nursery and kindergarten groups are: doll clothes, doll bed linens and table linens, clothes for dramatic play (from adults' clothes), stuffed animals, animal cages, drums and other musical instruments.

Games and equipment can be made easily, also.

Games

Beanbags. Shelled corn makes a light filler. The bags need to be filled half full so that little hands can throw and catch them more easily. An outer covering which is washable should be made. Inner tubes which have been inflated and placed flat on the ground make good receptacles into which the beanbags may be tossed.

Fishing game. Fish may be made of colored paper with paper-clip noses added. Short fishing poles made of small dowels, and a small magnet tied on the end of the line as a hook will provide lots of fun for children as they fish from their "boats on their river."

Tenpins or Bowling game. Paper milk cartons make good tenpins. A small rubber ball can be used to knock over the pins.

Equipment

Clay boards. One-inch boards, well-sanded and corners rounded, may be shellacked and then waxed. A good size is 12" x 15".

Insect cages. Materials needed for making a small insect cage are two round 8-inch cake pans and a strip of screen wire, 10" x 30". Roll the screen wire to fit tightly into the cake pan, fasten at top and bottom with stapler or paper clips. Then place other cake pan over the top of the roll of wire as a lid.
Another type of cage for insects can be made with a large lamp chimney and a piece of screen wire cut to fit the top. Adhesive tape will keep it in place. A small potted plant may be used as the food for the insects. Place glass chimney over the plant and press down into soil ½ inch to hold it in place.

Dollhouses. Cardboard cartons from the grocery make nice-sized rooms for a dollhouse. The inside may be papered with wallpaper from discarded sample books. The outside may be painted with tempera paint to cover the advertising. Paper gummed tape may be used to bind the rough edges of the box and give it a finished look. The doll furniture may be made from scraps and waste materials such as spools, small waxed milk cartons, paper ice cream dishes, ribbon spools, salt boxes, colored cupcake papers, lace, cloth, small cardboard cartons. A little ingenuity, paste, brads, needle and thread, and behold, the house is beautifully furnished. Wooden people or people cut out of mail-order catalogs or pattern books may live happily in such a home.

Stick horses. Very realistic horses may be made from the following materials: broom handle, man's plain cotton sock, old felt hat, colored twill tape, tar tape, cotton or old nylon hose, two buttons, and two small plastic rings.
Stuff the sock tightly with cotton or nylon hose, or both. Pad well the end of the broom handle before inserting it into the neck of the horse so that it will not punch through the top of the horse's head. Finish stuffing the neck, smoothing it around carefully. Gather the top of the sock together at the base of the horse's neck and tie securely. A few tacks will make it more secure. Then wrap tar tape around this part of the neck until the tacks and sock are covered. Sew on the ears and mane cut from the discarded felt hat. (Velour hats make beautiful ears and mane.) Then sew on the bridle of twill tape. Attach the rings on either side of the horse's mouth and sew the reins

into them. Embroidered nose and colored buttons for eyes give personality to the horse.

Dolly for clay container. Platform with ball-bearing casters. Small cleats nailed down hold the container in place.

Wooden ramp. A wooden ramp makes running and play with wheel toys more interesting. It may be built the desired height (8″ or 10″) and 5′ or 6′ wide. The ramps on either side of the platform need to be long enough so that the incline is not too steep.

Climbing tunnels. Long, substantial, smooth-finished barrels with both ends removed can be made into climbing tunnels. Strong lumber for the frames, two wooden ladders, and a 10″ board for sliding are all that is needed to produce an intriguing piece of climbing apparatus.

Large domino blocks (for older five's). Twenty-eight smooth blocks, 6″ x 3″, make up a set of double-six dominoes. The dots may be burned or painted on and then covered with two coats of clear varnish.

Steering wheel in block. A steering wheel may be obtained from a local automobile garage. A frame box may be made into which the steering wheel is connected. It can be used for a bus, car, tractor, truck, jeep, or boat in dramatic play. Paint will make it more durable for outdoor play.

Wall easels. To conserve floor space, easels may be made and attached to the wall. Hinges may be used to allow the easels to stand out from the wall. The paint trays should be removable so that when the easels are not in use they may fold flat against the wall.

Scrap Materials

The resourceful teacher helps children and parents find constructive uses for a wide variety of scrap materials. The following are some of the materials which can be conserved for creative use in nursery and kindergarten groups:

newspapers (protection of easels, tables, and other work spaces)
magazines (pictures for various needs)
wooden buckets, kegs, large fiber containers (drums, storage containers)
broom handles (rhythm sticks, stick horses)
turkey feathers, discarded silk scarfs (rhythms)
gourds (rattles for rhythmic play, maracas)
discarded polyethylene containers, squeeze bottles, etc. (water and sand play)
scrap cloth (doll clothes, beanbag covers, discovering feel of different materials)
scrap wood (woodwork activities)

cartons of all sizes (dramatic play, rooms for dollhouse, storage)

wooden boxes, crates (animal cages, dramatic play outdoors)

copper wire (Christmas tree decorations)

large thread cones (dramatic play, sand play)

small cardboard boxes with clear plastic tops (displaying collections of seeds, shells, rocks, and other "treasures" from nature)

pine cones, large seed pods (Christmas tree decorations)

string, yarn, ribbon, buttons, rickrack (making collage creations)

cardboard (art activities such as mounting pictures and for collages)

popsicle sticks (paste sticks)

egg cartons (making collections of seeds or other interesting findings on a nature walk)

food cans with bottoms cut out, food cartons (dramatic play in home center and grocery store)

#10 food cans (art activities)

milk cartons (containers for paint, planting seeds, store and home play, boats for water play)

round, pint-size ice cream cartons (hand rattlers, toy telephones, bubble-blowing)

gallon jars with lids (terrarium)

wallpaper, wallpaper sample books (decorative purposes, papering dollhouse rooms, covering dollhouse furniture)

pieces of garden hose (water play, dramatic play—as fire truck equipment)

rubber tubing (water play, siphoning)

old clocks, locks and keys (experimentation)

cottage cheese containers (bubble-blowing containers)

men's and women's apparel and accessories (dress-up box)

old plastic drapes, tablecloths, shower curtains (aprons for water play)

corrugated paper (mounting pictures, collages, pencil holders—2" strips rolled up and fastened with strip of wallpaper)

aluminum frozen food pie plates, TV dinner plates (paste containers on table, sand and water play, exhibiting "treasures" in science center, serving meals on an airplane in dramatic play, having TV dinner in playhouse)

pattern books (paper dolls for dollhouse, making family books)

inner tubes (outdoor play—rolling tube, stepping from one to another, throwing beanbags into center when tube is lying flat)

Sources of Equipment

Illustrated equipment catalogs may be secured on request from the following companies:

1. Atlanta Toy Company
   951 Peachtree Battle Circle, N. W.
   Atlanta, Georgia
2. Childcraft Equipment Company
   155 East 23rd Street
   New York 10, N. Y.
3. Community Playthings
   Rifton, New York
4. Creative Playthings
   5 University Place
   New York 3, N. Y.
5. Educational Equipment Company
   New York 10, N. Y.
6. Fox Blocks Company
   24401 Redwood Highway
   Cloverdale, Calif.
7. The Judy Company
   310 N. Second Street
   Minneapolis 1, Minn.
8. Seaver Toy Company
   3050 N. Lima
   Burbank, Calif.
9. Society for Visual Education
   Chicago, Ill. (Educational Film-strips Catalog)
10. R. H. Stone Products
    P. O. Box 414
    Detroit 31, Mich.
11. Strombeck-Becker Manufacturing Company
    Department E.
    Moline, Ill.
12. Children's Reading Service
    1078 St. John's Place
    Brooklyn 13, N. Y.
13. Children's Record Guild
    Young People's Records
    The Greystone Corporation
    100 Sixth Ave.
    New York 13, N. Y.

Bibliography for Standards

1. Association for Childhood Education International, 3615 Wisconsin Ave., N. W., Washington 16, D. C.
   A. C. E. I., *Portfolio for Kindergarten Teachers.*
   A. C. E. I., *Portfolio on More and Better Schools for Children Under Six.*
   A. C. E. I., *Nursery School Portfolio.*
   A. C. E. I., *Creating With Materials for Work and Play.*
   A. C. E. I., *Equipment and Supplies.*
2. *Education for Children Below Six* (Planning for America's Children Series). National Council of State Consultants in Elementary Education, in care of Miss Elsie Schneider, Boston House, 1711 Massachusetts Ave., N. W., Washington, D. C., 1955.
3. Many State Departments of Education have bulletins which give standards, legislation, and state regulations for nursery schools and kindergartens.

Chapter III

Looking at Young Children

Age Developmental Characteristics

In order to plan adequately for the school environment, appropriate guidance, and worthwhile experiences for young children, teachers must gain insights and understanding of the stages of developmental growth of children under six.

Although we are aware of the fact that each child is a unique individual—that no two children are alike—we recognize that there are certain characteristics which children have in common at about the same age. These cannot be considered with precise expectation according to the child's chronological age, for growth and development have the qualities of both "has been" and "becoming," and each child follows his own pattern and rate of growth.

Therefore, in looking at the following brief age descriptions of young children, teachers must view them only as an aid to their study of young children and not as a yardstick for measuring and evaluating the growth and development of the Anns, Tonys, Dicks, and Susans in their nursery or kindergarten groups.

Three-Year-Olds

The three-year-old is still an exceedingly self-centered individual, but he is gradually recognizing his place in his home in relation to the other members of his family. He is beginning to play *with* other children, not always *parallel to* them.

He is apt to be possessive of other children's toys and he seems to think in terms of ownership of those which he particularly desires. If force is necessary to get possession of a toy or a piece of play equipment, he will use it with no inhibitions—shoving, pushing, hitting, or even biting and kicking to gain his objective.

His life is filled with many imaginary experiences and playmates. He can control such situations and playmates and never be threatened by them. However, he finds difficulty often in separating reality from the products of his imagination.

The three-year-old child's vocabulary is limited, but he enters into much more conversation than he did as a two-year-old. He is beginning to use silly language rather fluently as he tries out various vocal sound effects.

His interest span is quite short, particularly with reference to listening activities, but he can concentrate on play with other children for somewhat longer blocks of time than the two-year-old.

The three-year-old has difficulty in coping with frustrations. He will laugh, scream, pout, or have a vigorous tantrum all within a brief span of a morning. His lack of experience in knowing the acceptable ways of making social contacts causes him to experiment with all kinds of responses. He may fling out in all directions, or withdraw quietly; snatch and grab, or retreat leaving the toy in dispute; seek constant approval and help from the teacher, or ignore adults completely. In his play he dramatizes life around him as he sees it. He loses himself completely in the role he adopts, so intent is he in his play. And he may change his role momentarily without warning.

The three-year-old is developing motor skills quite rapidly; he enjoys large-muscle play and displays improved co-ordination in his running, climbing, walking, and riding a tricycle.

Four-Year-Olds

The four-year-old is living through a period of accelerated activity, both physical and mental. He is an eager *"doer"* and a perpetual "questioner." He seeks, explores, and investigates wherever he is. He is a very literal-minded being, living in the *here and now*.

He enjoys motor activities involving the whole body and is rapidly gaining skill in locomotion, particularly in his walking and running ability. He is adept with his hands, but is unequal to tasks requiring small-muscle control. He shows an increase in the length of his attention span, but as yet he can engage in listening activities for only a few minutes at a time.

His increase in language usage is quite apparent. He is losing his baby ways of verbalization. He can understand more complex directions and conversations. And he revels in nonsense language. As he experiments with vocal sounds he creates strange, meaningless words. A four-year-old will frequently take a person's name and create rhyming words as Donny did with "Miss Lilly." Donny kept saying over and over, "Miss Lilly, Miss Lilly, that's silly, willy, pilly, Billy, hilly, killy, Miss Lilly." Often his conversation becomes exceedingly silly and nonsensical.

Much of his play is still imaginary and dramatic. Although he plays with other children, it is on a very loosely organized basis. Much of his play is still parallel to his playmates. At times, however, his play shows responses which indicate the beginnings of co-operation. His play is loud and boisterous and filled with big talk, quarreling, name-calling, and other socially disapproved responses. He becomes angry at his peers, but recovers quickly and will rejoin the group to continue the play as though there had never been a storm. He seems able to go out of bounds with apparent ease.

The four-year-old seems to have renewed zeal to achieve more and more independence. This accounts for his frequent resistance to those necessary limits placed on his freedom. However, after the "scene of resistance" has passed, he usually appreciates the security which those limits ensure him.

Five-Year-Olds

The five-year-old enjoys good general health, but he is still subject to communicable diseases. He has not lived long enough yet to build up the immunity which he will later enjoy.

His gross motor activity is quite well developed by age five. He can walk and run with good co-ordination. He can climb and descend steps and skip, alternating his feet with comparative ease.

The five-year-old has usually established his handedness. He knows the hand with which he paints, draws, and cuts, although he may not be able to identify the right and left members of his body. His eye-hand co-ordination is well-developed, yet he is not able to perform tasks requiring fine-muscle usage.

The five-year-old is quite active, although he may appear more restrained in his activity than the four-year-old. This may be due to the fact that he can remain with one activity longer or can play longer in a given area than he could as a four-year-old. His play, however, is vigorous and noisy. It is taking on purpose, and a bit of organization is apparent as a child will direct "who" each is to be and "where."

He enjoys his play with other children and is beginning to display some ability to co-operate with his peers. Much of his play is made up of the dramatic, imaginative type. He plays out situations which he knows and situations which may have been puzzling to him. This is one of his methods for understanding better his environment and the experiences with which he is faced. Playing the role of doctor when the dolls are sick helps him to have a better relationship with his own doctor when later he may need a shot or other medical care.

The five-year-old is quite a conversationalist, but he is apt to make unreliable statements because of his lack of command of language. He enjoys stories and will listen to them over and over again. He doesn't mind as much as he did having the details of the story changed on him. He prefers, however, stories about the here and now. Fairy tales hold little attraction for him, for he is still such a literal-minded person. He enjoys a good joke on someone else but he cannot yet appreciate a joke on himself. For the most part, he is full of good humor much of the time.

He is becoming a well-poised being who likes to feel helpful to those around him. He can and does assume simple responsibilities in his home and at school. He is beginning to respect individuals and their rights. He demands respect from others with regard to his property rights, for he has a rather exaggerated sense of ownership.

The five-year-old bids for affection from adults and displays jealousy if he thinks he has competition for the affection he desires from the grownups in his life. At this age the child experiences a very real fear of losing his parents. Although he is striving hard to achieve more and more independence from his parents, he is especially attached to his mother, who supplies much of his physical needs. This is the age when the child has such bad dreams and even nightmares. The dreams usually contain wild animals and strange people chasing the child or harming him in some gruesome manner.

The five-year-old enjoys a routine and has little trouble adjusting to a program of activities which allows freedom of selection and yet maintains a consistent sequence of activities.

Altogether, parents and teachers generally consider that of all early childhood, five is the most interesting age and the easiest with which to live.

Implications for Teachers of Young Children

Recognizing that in many respects young children of about the same age have many growth characteristics in common, the teacher may plan more adequately for appropriate group experiences for her children:

1. Knowing that young children are very active, the teacher will

provide adequate space indoors and out. She will "take stock" of all the furniture and large equipment to ascertain the importance of the role which they play in the "good life" of the young child at school. This may mean that in order to give the children enough floor space some of the tables and chairs should be dispensed with. It also means that the equipment should be movable and of the type which can be used creatively by the group in a number of different ways, allowing freedom for action.

2. The teacher, aware of the fact that young children's play is vigorous, will provide large, sturdy equipment for climbing, balancing, and riding, and also places for digging. She will also plan opportunities for rhythmic activities of running, hopping, skipping, dancing, galloping, and many other bodily expressions which the children enjoy inventing as they interpret music.

3. The teacher knows that because the children's large muscles are developing first, she needs to provide for them large play and work materials; that is, large balls, large blocks, large chunks of clay, large crayons and chalk, large paintbrushes, and large sheets of paper on which to express their thoughts and feelings. She will see that the children at school do not have activities which call for eye-hand co-ordination requiring fine-muscle usage, such as "coloring in" pictures, cutting out intricate figures, using small peg boards, working with sewing cards, and the like.

4. Knowing that young children spend much time in dramatizing life about them, the teacher will provide an abundance of resource materials for enriching the children's play. This will mean, besides the equipment in the home and block center, having a box of interesting dress-up clothes and play accessories such as a fireman's hat, doctor's kit, toy cash register, large flat paintbrushes and painter's cap, squares of cloth, red bandanna handkerchiefs, tire pump, ad infinitum.

5. Recognizing that young children are becoming increasingly interested in and capable of working and playing together in small groups, the teacher will plan for and provide opportunities for them to work and play with a few friends of their own choosing. (She will not "require" real co-operation of the children for she knows that the "i" in child is still a capital "I," but she can foster interest in small-group co-operative play.)

6. The teacher of young children, knowing that they are usually farsighted, will see that the children spend very little time looking closely at small things or engaging in fine work. She will arrange

the book center in a well-lighted area of the room in which there is no glare. She will have a variety of picture books with illustrations which are large and not too detailed.

7. Knowing that young children fatigue easily, the teacher will balance the active times with periods of quiet activities throughout the session, maintaining a consistent rhythm of both kinds of activities.

8. The teacher is continually aware of the evidence of the young child's growing independence. She will meet his need for doing things for himself by providing individual lockers for the child's personal things, child-size clean-up equipment easily accessible to him, and low shelves which make it possible for the child to select the materials or toys he wishes, and likewise to put them away without adult help. She will allow for individual responsibility in habits of toileting and hand-washing and in participation in such room routines as pouring the juice, watering the flowers, and feeding the pets.

9. Realizing that young children are curious and full of questions, the teacher will provide materials which will inspire and challenge them to make discoveries and find answers to some of their own questions by experimenting and problem-solving. She will encourage discussion in group planning and evaluation of the children's work. She will create an environment in which the children feel free to communicate their thoughts and feelings. And she will encourage growth in the children's vocabulary by enriching their environment through firsthand and vicarious experiences.

10. Being aware of the young child's capacity for wonder and awe, the teacher is sensitive to the child's responses and will provide opportunities for spontaneous worship in the group as she recognizes his readiness for such experiences.

11. Knowing that young children need assurance that they are loved and needed and valued as individuals, the teacher will provide a warm, friendly, challenging, and consistent environment in which the children live and learn together.

Providing for Individual Differences

The teacher, aware of the general likenesses among young children, is also keenly concerned about the differences in each individual making up the group.

1. She knows that although there is a difference in chronological

age of only a few months, there are wide differences in physical growth, mental ability, and social and emotional maturity within the group. She will be constantly aware of differences in interest and performance, language usage, creative expression, imagination, sensory perception, and behavior in problem-solving situations. This means that adaptations and adjustments will be necessary in the curriculum and in the equipment used.

2. To take care of background differences the teacher will set up centers of interest which change with the interests and needs of individuals and the group. As a group works in building a center of interest, other children will be attracted to the activity. Each child contributes according to his ability, growing as an individual in a functioning group. The teacher will see to it that each child has some opportunity to "shine" and to realize a personal pride in the success of his undertaking.

3. If there is a child in the group with a physical handicap, care must be taken that activities are provided in which he can happily participate. The teacher will help him to enjoy achievement in ways in which he is physically capable. She will also be alert to help the group understand and accept the handicapped child as the need arises. With the child whose hearing is poor, the teacher will want to watch to see that the child is in front of and near the one who is telling or reading a story to the group. She may need to encourage the child to play with other children in small groups, for many times the hard-of-hearing child will become withdrawn from the group.

4. For the immature child, the teacher will need to adapt the activities so that this child can do other things with a sense of satisfaction without disturbing the rest of the group.

Whatever the child's difficulty, the teacher will strive to help him develop a mental outlook and forms of response which will make for his own happiness and his social adjustment in his group.

As the teacher recognizes the differences which make each child a unique person, she will plan the curriculum to best meet the developmental needs and interests of the individuals. With respect for the individual, she will give each child the affection, security, and guidance he needs in proportion to his needs.

The teacher will accept each child where he is in his development. She takes into account the fact that growth is gradual but continuous and that each child has his own rate of growth and pattern which he follows. So with patience and understanding she seeks ever to provide an educational environment and a program which stimulate and promote the realization of each child's full potential at his present stage of maturity.

Bibliography for Looking at Young Children

Baruch, Dorothy, *Understanding Young Children*. New York: Teacher's College, Columbia University, 1949.

Child Development Guides For Teachers of Three, Four, and Five-Year-Old Children. New York State Education Department, Albany, New York.

Cohen, Dorothy H. and Stern, Virginia, *Observing and Recording the Behaviour of Young Children*. Bureau of Publications, Teacher's College, Columbia University, 1958.

Edwards, Morton, *Your Child Today*. New York: Permabooks, 1960.

Forest, Ilse, *Child Development*. New York: McGraw-Hill Book Co., 1954.

Fraiberg, Selma, *The Magic Years—Understanding and Handling the Problems of Early Childhood*. New York: Charles Scribner's Sons, 1959.

Gesell, Arnold, *et al., The First Five Years of Life*. New York: Harper & Brothers, 1940.

Havighurst, Robert J., *Developmental Tasks and Education*. New York: Longmans, Green & Co., Inc., 1952.

Hurlock, Elizabeth, *Child Growth and Development*. New York: McGraw-Hill Book Co., 1956.

Hurlock, Elizabeth, *Child Development*. New York: McGraw-Hill Book Co., 1956.

Hymes, James L., Jr., *A Child Development Point of View*. New York: Prentice-Hall, Inc., 1955.

Hymes, James L., Jr., *Understanding Your Child*. New York: Prentice-Hall, Inc., 1952.

Jenkins, Gladys, *These Are Your Children*. New York: Scott Whitman, 1953. Enlarged Edition.

Jersild, Arthur, *Child Development and the Curriculum*. New York: Teacher's College, Columbia University, 1949.

Landreth, Catherine, *The Psychology of Early Childhood*. New York: Alfred A. Knopf, Inc., 1958.

Redl, Fritz, *Understanding Children's Behavior*. New York: Teacher's College, Columbia University, 1957.

Sherrill, Lewis J., *Understanding Children*. New York: Abingdon Press, 1939.

Spock, Benjamin, *Pocket Book of Baby and Child Care*. Pocket Books, Inc., 1946, revised 1960.

Strang, Ruth, *Introduction to Child Study*. New York: The Macmillan Company, 1952, 1959.

U. S. Dept. of Health, Education, and Welfare, *Your Child From One to Six*.

Witmer, H. L. and Kotinsky, Ruth, editors, *Personality in the Making*. New York: Harper & Brothers, 1952.

Wolf, Anna W. and Szasz, Susanne, *Helping Your Child's Emotional Growth*. New York: Doubleday & Company, Inc., 1955.

Sources of Pamphlets:

A Healthy Personality for Your Child. Discussion Guide for this pamphlet. James L. Hymes, Jr., Federal Security Agency. Children's Bureau, Washington, D. C.

Teacher, Listen, the Children Speak. James L. Hymes, Jr., New York State Committee on Mental Hygiene, 105 East 22nd Street, New York.

Aggressiveness in Children. Edith Lesser Atkin, and staff of Child Study Association. Child Study Publications. The Child Study Association of America, Inc., 132 East 74th Street, New York 21, N. Y.

How Children Grow and Develop. Willard Olson and John Lewellen.

Understanding Hostility in Children. Science Research Associates, Inc., 57 West Grand Ave., Chicago 10, Ill.

Helping Children Grow. Association for Childhood Education International, 3615 Wisconsin Ave., N. W., Washington 16, D. C.

How Do Your Children Grow? Association for Childhood Education International.

Chapter IV

Health Education in the Nursery-Kindergarten Program

Mental Health

Helping young children to acquire and maintain mental-emotional health is one of the teacher's chief concerns. This can be realized as she creates a wholesome emotional climate in the classroom and controls the conditions which help the children to meet satisfactorily their psychological needs for belonging, participation, accomplishment, status, and security.

The teacher's own attitude and approach in the group is important in establishing the kinds of teacher-pupil relationships and pupil-pupil relationships which are conducive to good mental-emotional health. As young children enter nursery school or kindergarten, they need a great deal of assurance of acceptance and much support from an understanding teacher. She will respect and warmly accept each child *as he is* and *where he is* in his total development, and will help him to accept and appreciate himself. She will also help each child to feel a sense of adequacy because his *best efforts* are considered worthwhile and are evaluated only from the standpoint of his present level of ability and development. This may sometimes be accomplished for individuals as the teacher gives a smile, a nod of approval, or a pat on the back. Occasionally just patient, attentive listening to a child will give him the support he needs at the particular time. Praise, which is to help in meeting the young child's emotional needs, must be given *for the child himself*. Praise which stimulates competition within the group can only be harmful emotionally to the individual receiving the praise and to the rest of the group. It endangers teacher-pupil and pupil-pupil relationships as well, and sets up standards of behavior and performance which might be out of reach for some of the youngsters in the group.

There should be plenty of opportunities for children to "play out" their feelings and get release from their tensions in socially accept-able ways. This means that there will be clay to beat and punch, finger paint to squish and squash, easel paints to use on large pieces of paper as the child's feelings dictate, wood on which to hammer and saw, a digging spot in the play area, and perhaps a small punching bag or large rag doll. The teacher is not dealing in "play therapy," but the environment she creates in the school can have therapeutic values for the children.

It is equally important for the group to be able to let off steam at times to maintain the right "emotional temperature" in the room. Careful planning of the group's activities for the day will help to lessen the possibilities of tension in the group. Frequent times of rest and quiet alternating with periods of activity will reduce the possibility of fatigue. But when tensions do become evident in the group, as they will at times, the teacher can help the children find release by guiding the group in a lively singing game or some vigorous rhythms.

The teacher will remember that each child develops at his own pace and cannot be pushed or hurried in his growth without doing injury to his emotional well-being. She will be consistent in ex-pecting good living, and will maintain an objective, friendly attitude in dealing with misbehavior. She will exercise great care in being certain that each child, no matter what he does, can feel that he is loved and is an accepted member of the group.

"Before a child goes to school he looks to the parent for support and praise. You hear him say, 'My mother says . . .' or 'My father says. . . .' After he has been in school for a time and feels loved and accepted by the teacher who helps him learn and succeed, he adds another person to this list and you hear him say, 'My teacher says. . . .' The necessity for harmony and unity between home and school can, therefore, be seen. Since both parent and teacher are significant in his life, and since he has had very limited experience, he looks to them for strength, approval, and guidance."[1] Therefore, "Teachers of young children need to know their parents and their environ-mental influences so they will not needlessly cause them confusion, unhappiness, and emotional disturbance. Teachers and parents should know each other as interested partners in the process of helping the children feel secure in their acceptance of them, their home, and their school."[2]

The teacher must be a well-adjusted, mature adult herself, with a calm, quiet, well-modulated voice. Her unhurried manner rubs off on the children, lessening the possibility of tenseness in the group. A teacher whose radiant Christian faith shines through her every thought, word, and relationship in the group, inspires in the children confidence and trust, and helps them to gain status and emotional security.

Resulting from good group living in the kindergarten are the children's "healthy feelings about themselves and happy relationships with others"[3]—the basis for healthy mental and emotional development.

Some of the attitudes which make up the healthy personal feelings and result in happy relationships are:

"Feelings of personal worth and self-respect
Friendliness and consideration toward others (good manners)
Desire to plan and share group responsibilities and activities
Ability to take criticism without feeling hurt or inferior
Freedom from foolish fears
Self-confidence and increasing independence in:
    caring for himself
    helping others
    meeting new people and situations
    making choices suitable to his age
    accepting the results of his choices and actions
    solving his own problems."[4]

An excellent source of materials for teachers and for their use with parents of young children is the Department of Mental Health in each of the State Departments of Health located in each state capital. Many of the pamphlets which they distribute are free. The Departments of Mental Health also maintain free film libraries and will send teachers, upon request, listings of the films available and will help in scheduling films for use in their adult groups.

Rest and Relaxation

"The kindergarten, by providing rest periods and a program planned to give relaxation through change of activity, attempts to:
    Establish a balance between activity and quiet.
    Give the child a time of uninterrupted quiet.
    Help the child to learn to enjoy quiet.
    Teach the child how to relax.
    Really rest the child."[5]

Times of rest and relaxation may be either active or passive. Children are engaging in active rest when they are participating in such activities as group discussion, enjoying books or puzzles, listening to stories, and, perhaps, looking at a filmstrip. Passive rest is characterized by quiet and inactivity. It may follow any strenuous activity, but most teachers prefer to have a planned rest period usually following "juice time"—about midmorning. The length of time observed in the rest period in the group may vary from fifteen to twenty minutes. Some days the group will need a little longer rest time than usual. When the children understand that their rest time is consistently one of considerable length (15-20 minutes), they are usually willing to settle down and enjoy it. Occasionally, a child will become so relaxed that he drops off to sleep.

Preparation for Rest Time

1. Be sure there are no drafts in the room and that the temperature (on the child's level) is not lower than 68 degrees.
2. Have the children set up their cots (if that is the equipment used) or place their resting mats on the floor with ample space between each and arranged with the feet and heads alternating.
3. See that each child is covered with his own thin blanket.
4. Turn out the lights and draw the shades or close the blinds.
5. Soft music may be played to help create a restful atmosphere.
6. Sometimes a story may be read as the group rests.
7. The teacher stays seated during rest time after she sees that everyone is comfortable and settled.

If children have difficulty in relaxing, they might be encouraged and helped in the following ways:

A bit of imitative play may be employed. The children can pretend they are trees swaying and bending their bodies—swinging their arms back and forth like branches as the wind blows heavily.

They may, in autumn, imitate the falling leaves, twirling, fluttering to the ground as the wind calls them to play.

If there is a big rag doll in the kindergarten, the teacher may demonstrate how the doll stands and sits in its floppy way. The children will enjoy letting themselves go limp until they are finally relaxed and ready to rest.

Sometimes the teacher may move about the room quietly as the children are getting settled on their mats and sing softly a resting song. The following is the type of song which encourages quiet rest.

RESTING TIME

(*Tune: Brahms' "Lullaby"*)
Resting time is quiet time;
We have stopped all our play.
We will lie down on our mats (cots),
It's our quiet time of day.

Resting time is sleepy time;
We are quiet at rest.
Resting time is sleepy time;
We will close our eyes and rest.

Incidental Resting

Resting should certainly not be limited to the one scheduled time of the morning. When fatigue is manifested by the loss of emotional control, by the use of high-pitched voices, loud, boisterous laughter, and general restlessness in the group, the teacher will find that providing an opportunity for resting will help the children get back on an even keel.

Safety

Since safety is an essential phase of daily living, safety education should provide children "with the knowledge, understanding, skills, habits, and attitudes that will enable them to live vigorously and happily and at the same time safely."[6]

To be effective in realizing safe living in the group and proper guidance in safety education for the children, the teacher would want to set up some specific objectives such as:

To help children establish habits and attitudes that will make for safe living in the group.

To help children attain behavior patterns which will contribute to their own personal safety and the safety of those about them at school and at home.

To provide a lush environment of varied firsthand experiences which will allow the children to use safety understandings, habits, skills, and attitudes in a natural, positive manner.

Safety of the children is the primary concern of the teacher at all times. In other words:

She knows where the children are and what they are doing every minute of the session;

She keeps a careful check on all equipment to be certain there are not splinters, sharp edges, or broken parts which would be dangerous;

She arranges the room and the outdoor play area in such a way that the most active areas have more space and offer the least opportunity for collision; and

She encourages the children in their play with such remarks as "Hold tightly," "Use both hands," rather than startling them with remarks such as "Be careful, don't fall," or "Look out, don't go so high."

"Safety education is not a separate subject; it permeates the entire curriculum. . . . Children learn safe ways of living when safety instruction is made a part of their actual life experiences and is adapted to their needs and interests."[7]

The following are a few suggestions of experiences which may be planned with kindergarten children:

1. Becoming acquainted with some of the community helpers in safety.
2. Visiting a fire station.
3. Having a policeman visit the group.
4. Dramatizing ways the policeman helps people.
5. Learning full name, telephone number, and address.
6. Learning the safe way to use scissors, carry chairs, play with the large blocks, and play in the sandbox.
7. Making a few necessary safety rules for the use of the wheel toys.
8. Practicing fire drills so that a real one will not be a frightening experience.
9. Hearing stories about safe work and play.
10. Singing songs about safe ways at work and play.

In the event of an accident, the teacher needs to remain calm and maintain an attitude of assurance. She should render the necessary first aid and contact the child's parents and doctor in case of serious accident. She should always report to the child's mother any accident, no matter how seemingly minor it may be. She should explain the first aid rendered. A complete record of the accident should be made and kept in the child's file.

Children should be urged to tell the teacher when they have even the slightest injury and to co-operate with her in receiving the necessary first-aid treatment.

Accidents cannot always be prevented. However, the teacher who is alert and is conscientiously concerned about the safety of her group will greatly limit the possibility of even minor accidents. She will remember that the children's health and safety are chief among her responsibilities toward them.

PUPIL ACCIDENT REPORT

Name _____   Home Address _____

School _____   Address _____

Time of Accident _____   Date of Accident _____

Place Accident Occurred _____

Description of Accident:

    Nature of injury _____

    What was the child doing? _____

    How did it happen? _____

Estimate of Injury:

    Stayed at home _____   Sent to doctor _____

    Sent home _____   Sent to hospital _____

Teacher in charge when accident occurred   Present at scene of accident:

_____   Yes _____   No _____

Name of person administering first aid   Treatment given: _____

_____   _____

Notification of:

    Parents _____   By _____

    Name of doctor _____   By _____

    Name of hospital _____   By _____

Witnesses:

Name _____   Address _____

Name _____   Address _____

Recommendations for preventing other accidents of this type:

_____

_____

_____

_____

_____

_____

_____

_____

Signed _____

Weekday Church School Teacher

Body Functions

Care of Eyes

In helping young children to learn to care for their eyes, the teacher will be certain, first of all, that the school environment provides the physical essentials for protecting children's eyes. This means a well-lighted room with 20-40 foot-candle light in all parts of the room and the absence of glare. It will mean also that in group activities such as story time, the children will sit with their backs to the light. And it means constant vigil on the part of the teacher for identifying hazards to eyes in the children's work and play in the playroom and out-of-doors.

Children need help in learning to keep their hands and objects away from their eyes. They need to learn how and why they should use scissors properly. They need encouragement to play carefully in the sandbox. And they will need frequent reminders that sticks and sharp objects are not toys for safe players.

The teacher will not provide activities which call for close work such as small pegboards, small-detailed pictures, or sewing cards, because she knows that the young child is farsighted and that his eyes are not yet fully developed. Young children must be protected from eyestrain.

Care of Ears

Many young children experiment with their ears. They find them interesting to poke with their fingers or with objects, and also a convenient place to hide small things such as buttons and beans. Guidance in the care of ears needs to be individual as the need arises, otherwise some children might get a new idea for exploration if the subject came out in group discussion.

It is well, however, to help the children, through group activities, to understand the necessity of wearing a cap or ear muffs to cover their ears when they go outdoors on a cold, windy day. Making a practice of this at school is a part of learning to live healthfully day by day.

Care of the Teeth

Children will take great pride in their teeth if they are given proper encouragement at home and at school. The habits of care for their teeth must be formed at home, but the teacher can give support to the home activities by helping the children in their attitudes toward having a healthy mouth.

Through the use of pictures and stories, the children will be helped to feel good about their teeth, and will become increasingly interested in caring for them. They can begin to understand something of the significance of:

brushing their teeth twice a day;

letting the dentist help to keep their teeth "well" by visiting him twice a year, or as needed;

using only their own toothbrush;

never breaking hard objects such as candy, nuts, pencils, and the like with their teeth.

Elimination

At school the children should be free to use the bathroom facilities whenever they need to. They should be encouraged to go to the bathroom as soon as they feel the need and not play on and on as they are so prone to do.

At the beginning of the year, young children need guidance in the proper use of the school bathroom facilities. The habits of using toilet tissue and paper towels conservatively, flushing the toilet, and washing and drying their hands after toileting are very important parts of this routine. The development of healthy attitudes toward bodily eliminations are essential for attaining and maintaining optimum health. Children of this age are interested in their body and curious about its functions. They are apt to go on a "binge" of using "toilet vocabulary." The wise parent or teacher recognizes that they are acting their age and so ignores such conversation or just accepts it as any other conversation, knowing that it will pass in time if attention is not called to it.

Posture

Good posture contributes greatly to the growing child's good health. It increases his vigor, lessens fatigue, and aids his circulation and elimination. On the other hand, poor posture hinders the normal functions of the body, and, if not corrected, may be responsible for the development of certain physical defects.

Teachers of young children need to be aware of the principal causes of poor posture. Some of the more prominent causes are:

1. Weak, undeveloped muscles.
2. Improper or insufficient exercise.
3. Diseases such as tuberculosis, polio, and rickets.
4. Ill-fitting clothes, and shoes and socks which are too short.
5. Sitting in improperly fitted chairs, and having to sit in chairs too much.
6. General physical weakness due to malnutrition.
7. Fatigue.
8. Inability to accept self.
9. Emotional disturbance.
10. Continued unhappiness.

It is evident from the above-listed causes of poor posture that the teacher will not be able to help directly in the correction of every cause. But if she is sincerely concerned, she will find opportunities to work with the parents of children needing correction. If the problem of the young child's posture could be a subject for discussion at a mothers' meeting, it is likely that the mothers would approach the teacher about their own observations of their children's posture. Then, as a team—teacher and parent—they can face the child's difficulty and work together for the remedy.

Again as the teacher is trying to work for good posture, she must be a worthy example for the children to imitate. She can see that all the children have a chance to play on the climbing apparatus and with the other equipment for building large muscles. It is also the teacher's responsibility to create an environment which makes for happiness for *each child,* and one in which he feels accepted and needed as a participating member who makes worthy contributions to the group.

In planning for the activities of each day, the teacher is careful to guard against overstimulation, and balances rest with activity in the proportion needed by individuals and the group to avoid fatigue.

Included among the everyday experiences for young children is bodily rhythmic movement of the creative, dramatic type. This activity, joyous and free in character, develops not only motor co-ordination but also poise and posture, and serves to alleviate tensions.

Disease Prevention

Young children should never be made to feel anxious about sickness. They should not be continually reminded that if they fail to follow certain health practices they will surely get sick. But rather, the positive approach should be taken. Children should be helped to understand and appreciate the fact that keeping well will help them to grow.

Children attending nursery school and kindergarten should have received all the immunizations required for entrance to public school in the local community. Regulations of the local health board should be followed with regard to contagious diseases—that is, the incubation period and the length of time the child should be excluded from school when he has a communicable disease.

When children understand that the morning health inspection is primarily to help keep everyone well, they will usually co-operate with interest. The teacher or nurse should be as informal as possible in examining the children, chatting with them pleasantly and listening to their chatter, too. This takes their mind off of the routine. It is well for the parent or other person bringing the child to wait until the child's physical condition has been checked. This will eliminate making another trip to the school and will keep the child who must return home from having to wait. It makes having to go back home a little easier for the child, also.

The morning inspection will not guarantee that every child will be perfectly well all day. The teacher needs to be alert to symptoms which the children may evidence later on during the morning, for a child may seem hale and hearty at 9:00 A.M. and be running a fever or have a rash by 11:00 o'clock.

In the day-by-day living in the group the children should *begin to attain* the following habits and attitudes which will help in preventing disease:

1. Washing hands after toileting and before eating.
2. Keeping hands away from face.
3. Keeping fingers and toys out of mouth.
4. Drinking at the water fountain without touching the fixture with his mouth.
5. Not eating any food which has dropped to the floor.
6. Not eating part of another child's food.
7. Not exchanging clothes with other children.
8. Keeping his clothes and personal belongings in his own locker.
9. Covering coughs and sneezes with a handkerchief. (Paper hankies are more sanitary as they can be disposed of immediately after using.)
10. Showing the teacher any injury and telling her how it happened in case she did not see the accident.
11. Using paper handkerchief to get rid of sputum instead of spitting.

12. Co-operating happily with the teacher or nurse in morning health inspection.

Teaching young children the essentials of prevention of disease
is best done as the need arises in the natural setting of the occasion.
Again the positive approach is followed. Sometimes it will mean
individual or small-group guidance, and at other times group discussion, a story, or visual aids employed to help the child gain a
better understanding of the health problem involved. Here again, the
teacher's own good example in the group makes a tremendous
impact on the children and gives them an acceptable pattern to
emulate.

Cleanliness

Cleanliness as applied to the individual child means personal
cleanliness: clean, well-cared-for hair, a clean body, and clean
clothes. Much of the responsibility in this area rests on the child's
parents. However, young children can be encouraged at school to
have clean face, hands, neck, ears, and body. They can be helped
to appreciate and care for their clothes. Provision and encouragement
and guidance in hand-washing will build the proper attitude for
cleanliness as well as teach the correct use of water, soap, and towels.

Stories and pictures, along with occasional discussions and perhaps demonstrations with a doll, are methods effective in helping
young children enjoy and appreciate the need for bathing in their
homes.

Brushing teeth regularly is another health practice which has to
be done in the home, but interest and encouragement for regular
brushing of teeth and visits to the dentist can be given in the group.

Young children enjoy an attractive, well-kept playroom and will
react emotionally to it in being happier and more relaxed in their
work and play. Maintaining cleanliness of their environment is a
responsibility which the children should learn to share. Adequate
storage space, easily accessible to the children, encourages habits of
neatness and cleanliness.

If the children find their room each morning neat, orderly, and
inviting, they have a standard to work toward as they clean up after
their play and work activities. And if child-size clean-up equipment
is available, the children will be able to do a better job in straight-
ening the room. They thrive on the responsibility of being helpful.

The children should also take their share of responsibility in keeping the lavatory clean. They need help in learning to use the toilets properly, flushing after each use, and in the economical use of toilet tissue. They should learn to wash their hands under the running water in the basin. (If possible, the basins should be adjusted so that water cannot collect in them. This will make it impossible for several children to wash in the same water. It will also eliminate the hazard of a "flood" in the bathroom from an overflowing basin.)

Learning cleanliness is a part of the daily good living in the group. Teachers will remember that this age thrives on mess and "dirtiness." This natural drive should not be inhibited by an overemphasis on keeping things clean and in order. Young children can't grow as they should in a rigid, orderly, and spotless environment. They need to dabble and "mess" with finger paint, to pound and manipulate clay, to experiment and use easel paints, to dig in dirt and sand, and even to squish and squash in mud.

Then comes clean-up time.

Pictures, stories, poems, and songs help to create interest in the important business of cleanliness. Informal and incidental teaching in this area of health education probably ensures the most effective results. For example, after a good clean-up job, the teacher might suggest that the children look in the mirror and see what it tells them. She might chant the following to them:

> "Mirror, Mirror,
> What do you see?
> Little boy, little girl,
> As clean as can be.
> Mirror, Mirror,
> What do you see?
> Little boy, little girl
> Smiling at me."[8]

More than likely, the children will ask for it again and again and they will quickly make it a part of their repertoire of jingles. They may begin talking to the mirror themselves without suggestion from the teacher.

The simple little action song, "This Is the Way We Wash Our Hands," sung to the tune of "Here We Go 'Round the Mulberry Bush," is not only fun, but can stimulate interest in conversations about washing hands and face properly, or taking a good shower or tub bath. Stanzas may be created by the children and the song go on and on until they are "clean and dressed" from head to toe and ready for school.

Bibliography

A. S. C. D., *Health in Schools*. Department of N. E. A., Washington, D. C., 1951.

D'Evelyn, Katherine E., *Meeting Children's Emotional Needs*. Englewood Cliffs, N. J.: Prentice-Hall, Inc., 1957.

Edwards, Morton, editor, *Your Child from 2 to 5*. New York: Permabooks, 1955.

Federal Security Agency, *What Every Teacher Should Know About the Physical Condition of Her Pupils*. Pamphlet 68, 1945.

Federal Security Agency, *Teachers Contribute to Child Health*. Bulletin No. 8, 1951.

Foster, Josephine and Headley, Neith, *Education in the Kindergarten*. New York: American Book Company, 1948, revised 1959. Chapter XVI.

Heffernan, Helen, editor, *Guiding the Young Child*. Boston: D. C. Heath & Company, 1959.

Hymes, James L., Jr., *A Healthy Personality for Your Child*. Federal Security Agency, Children's Bureau, No. 337, 1952.

Hymes, James L., Jr., *A Pound of Prevention*. The New York State Society for Mental Health, 1954.

N. E. A. and A. M. A., *Health Education*. Department of N. E. A., Washington, D. C., 1955.

Ridenour, Nina and Johnson, Isabel, *Some Special Problems of Children Aged 2-5 Years*. New York: National Association for Mental Health, Inc., 1951.

Wills, Clarice and Stegeman, William, *Living in the Kindergarten*. Chicago: Follett Publishing Company, 1956.

Witmer, Helen and Kotinsky, Ruth, *Personality in the Making*. The Fact-Finding Report of the Mid-Century White House Conference on Children and Youth. New York: Harper & Brothers, 1952.

Wolf, Anna W. and Szasz, Suzanne, *Helping Your Child's Emotional Growth*. Garden City, New York: Doubleday & Company, Inc., 1954.

Health and Safety Books for Young Children

Berman, Rhoda, *When You Were a Little Baby*. New York: Lothrop, Lee & Shepard Co., Inc., 1954.

Brownell, Clifford and Evans, Ruth, *All Day, Every Day*. New York: American Book Company, 1954.

Brownell, Clifford and Williams, Jesse, *Well and Happy*. New York: American Book Company, 1946.

Irwin, Leslie W., Little, W. W., and Kelver, Caroline, *Awake and Away*. Chicago: Lyons & Carnahan, 1952.

Irwin, Leslie W., et al., *Growing Day by Day*. Chicago: Lyons & Carnahan, 1952.

Krauss, Ruth, *The Growing Story*. New York: Harper & Brothers, 1947.

Leaf, Munro, *Safety Can Be Fun*. Philadelphia: J. B. Lippincott Co., 1938.

Leaf, Munro, *Health Can Be Fun*. Philadelphia: J. B. Lippincott Co., 1943.

McKean, Elsie, *David's Bad Day*. New York: The Shady Hill Press, 1949.

Miner, Irene, *The True Book of Policemen and Firemen*. Chicago: Childrens Press, Inc., 1954.

Sources of Free and Inexpensive Health and Safety Education Materials

Bristol Myers Company, New York, N. Y.
John Hancock Mutual Life Insurance Company, 197 Clarendon Street, Boston, Mass.
Kellogg Company, Battle Creek, Michigan.
Metropolitan Life Insurance Company, 1 Madison Avenue, New York 10, N. Y.
National Dairy Health Council, 111 North Canal Street, Chicago, Ill.
Prudential Insurance Company of America. Local address.
State Board of Health in each state or Commonwealth.
U. S. Government Printing Office, Washington 25, D. C.

Chapter V

Special Days for Young Children

Halloween

Halloween is in the air for days before October 31st. The anticipation and planning for a special day often hold greater interest and value for the young child than the actual celebration itself.

There will be opportunities in the group for helping children deal with their fears of ghosts, witches, black cats, jack-o-lanterns, and goblins. Young children living in their realistic, here-and-now world sometimes find it hard to catch the spirit of these make-believe Halloween friends to whom older children have introduced them. The teacher will need to be aware of individual needs in this regard and make use of group discussion, funny Halloween stories, poems, songs, and dramatic play in order to alleviate the frightening element of the spookiness of Halloween.

There can be a variety of group activities for days in advance which will center around this festive day. A large calendar of October might be made with small paper pumpkins scotch-taped over the days of the month. Then each morning as a pumpkin is removed, the children can see that they are one day nearer to Halloween. The teacher may count aloud for the group the remaining pumpkins every few days. After several times, the children will be chiming in, counting along with the teacher and getting a feel for "time" as the days come and go. (No attempt is made to teach the children the numbers on the calendar, nor is this activity designed to teach them to count!)

This group will enjoy having a pumpkin or two in the room during the month, and then making jack-o-lanterns of them a few days before the celebration. (The teacher will always do the carving of the hat and face, but the children will enjoy scooping out the insides of the pumpkin, cleaning the slippery seeds and spreading them out to dry.) The jack-o-lantern must be lighted, of course, but a group discussion, with a little guidance, will usually result in the children banning the use of candles and suggesting flashl stead.

If it is possible for a group of the children to go to a gard farm nearby and select the pumpkins on the vine, it is much be .. If not, the teacher will need to have pictures of pumpkins growing in a field. Then in the spring the children can plant some of the seeds from their jack-o-lanterns in paper cups, watch them grow, and later transplant them outdoors at home. Who knows, they might be able to raise their own pumpkin for their next year's jack-o-lantern.

If a Halloween party is possible, it will involve the group in a variety of learning experiences. (Young children need real opportunities to do something helpful for someone else rather than participating in "Trick or Treat" activities or in minor neighborhood nuisance-activities on Halloween night.) The children may want to invite some grown-up friends to their party—perhaps members of the church staff or others who have had some previous association with the group. This will mean making and delivering or mailing invitations, planning and preparing the refreshments, making place mats, decorating napkins, and deciding on the kinds of activities they want to have at the party.

Some of the children's Halloween paintings will make interesting illustrated invitations. The teacher can manuscript the message as the children dictate it to her.

Making Jello is a simple but rewarding experience for little children. And what is prettier for a Halloween party than orange Jello? Icing cookies or graham crackers will give every child an opportunity to help with the refreshments. And anyway, pretty cookies just go with Jello at a party.

The teacher's ingenuity will be needed for providing simple games and activities which have a Halloween flavor. The following are original variations of a few finger plays and games with which kindergarten children may already be familiar:

Here's a Pumpkin (finger play)

Action. "Here's a pumpkin." (Thumb and index finger together.) "And here's a pumpkin." (Both hands together, thumb to thumb and index finger to index finger making a larger pumpkin.) "And a great big pumpkin we see." (Hands joined together forming a large circle with arms making the biggest pumpkin.) "Shall we count them? Here they are. One! Two! Three!" (Repeat each action in order on the counts, one, two, three.)

Two Halloween Owls (finger play)

Two Halloween owls looking at you,
One named Boo and one named Who.
Fly away Boo and fly away Who.
Come back Boo and come back Who.
Two Halloween owls looking at you.
One named Boo and one named Who.

This is a variation of the finger play, "Two little blackbirds sitting on a hill, One named Jack and one named Jill."
Tune. "Twinkle, Twinkle, Little Star."
Motion. In the first stanza raise index finger on each hand at "One named Boo and one named Who." For second stanza raise first two fingers on each hand while singing, "Four Halloween owls looking at you." Continue the song, adding one finger on each hand until there are ten Halloween owls.

Guess Who Has the Jack-O-Lantern? (recommended for older five's)

Formation. Children seated on the floor in a circle with their hands behind them.
Equipment. Small yellow paper or plastic jack-o-lantern.
Action. One child is chosen to sit in the center of the circle with his eyes closed. While the pianist plays a simple melody, the children pass the jack-o-lantern around the circle behind their backs. When the music stops, the child in the circle opens his eyes and tries to guess who has the jack-o-lantern. If he guesses correctly, the child who was holding the jack-o-lantern gets to hide his eyes and the game starts all over.

Guess What Is Missing?

Formation. Children informally grouped on the floor.
Equipment. Long, heavy string, five small metal clamps or clamp clothespins, and a picture of a witch, a black cat, a pumpkin, a jack-o-lantern, and a ghost. These may be cut out of colored paper so they can be more uniform in size.
Action. The clothesline may be strung up between two small chairs. The five pictures are clamped onto the clothesline. Everyone gets a good look at the arrangement. Then one child is chosen to be "it." He turns with his back to the clothesline and hides his eyes. Another child is chosen to remove one picture from the line. Then the child who is "it" tries to guess which picture is missing. The game may be played several times. Changing the position of the various pictures makes the game a little more challenging.

Five Little Jack-O-Lanterns (adaptation of "Five Little Chickadees")

Formation. Five small chairs placed in a row facing the children as they sit informally on the floor.

Action. Five children are chosen to be jack-o-lanterns and sit on the chairs. They act out the song the group sings:

Five little jack-o-lanterns looking in the door,
One ran away and then there were four.

(Refrain)
Jack-o-lantern, jack-o-lantern happy and gay,
Jack-o-lantern, jack-o-lantern run away.

Four little jack-o-lanterns sitting by a tree,
One ran away and then there were three.

(Refrain)

Three little jack-o-lanterns looking at you,
One ran away and then there were two.

(Refrain)

Two little jack-o-lanterns sitting in the sun;
One ran away and then there was one.

(Refrain)

One little jack-o-lantern left all alone,
He ran away and then there was none.

(Refrain)

One group of children changed the words to a simple singing game which they enjoyed, and created another Halloween game.

Pumpkin Yellow (see page 128 for melody)

Formation. Children stand in a circle facing the child who is chosen to be Pumpkin Yellow.

Action. Children join hands and walk around the circle as they sing the first stanza:

What can you do, Pumpkin Yellow, funny fellow?
What can you do, Pumpkin Yellow, funny you?

Child in center begins some action as jumping up and down, twirling around, tapping his feet, etc., while the group claps and sings:

> That's very fine, Pumpkin Yellow, funny fellow.
> That's very fine, Pumpkin Yellow, funny you.

As the children sing the next stanza, they imitate the child in the center of the circle:

> We'll do it too, Pumpkin Yellow, funny fellow.
> We'll do it too, Pumpkin Yellow, funny you.

As the group sings the last stanza the child in the center of the circle chooses another child to take his place:

> Whom do you choose, Pumpkin Yellow, funny fellow?
> Whom do you choose, Pumpkin Yellow, funny you?

Young children delight in creating their own spooky Halloween stories or making up an ending to a Halloween incident begun by the teacher. For example, the teacher might begin a story:

Once upon a time there was a very small pumpkin who lived in Farmer Brown's pumpkin patch. He had many pumpkin friends living in the same field. One day in October a man came to Farmer Brown's farm in a big truck. He wanted to buy Farmer Brown's pumpkins to take to the city to sell for Halloween.

The little pumpkin could hear the men talking as they walked around through the vines selecting the pumpkins that were to go to the city and become jack-o-lanterns for Halloween. He kept waiting for the men to come over to his vine and pick him. How he did want to go with his pumpkin friends in the truck to the city! If he could only be a jack-o-lantern and make the children laugh and shout on Halloween. But the big truck drove away without him. The little yellow pumpkin was very sad, but not for long, because . . .

Halloween noisemakers are fun to make and use. Small metal cans with lids that fasten tightly will be needed. A few very small pebbles, shelled corn, or acorns will make an interesting rattle. It may be decorated in any way that the child chooses.

Paper masks are not practical. Those made of paper sacks which pull over the child's head are responsible for injuries from falls or from the child's bumping into objects due to reduced vision. But the children can make funny faces on large paper sacks and have lots of fun with them. The twenty-pound paper bag from the grocery store is a good size. *Directions for funny face:* Open the bag and stuff it firmly with wads of newspaper, leaving about six or eight inches at the open end for pulling together and making a handle. Insert a piece of broom handle the desired length and tie the neck end of the sack head tightly around it. Then with pieces of colored paper or other scraps the child may make his spook's facial features. Paper or cloth strips make interesting hair. Some children may prefer to paint the face of their spook. An old hat fitted on the spook's head adds character to its personality. After making the spook, the child will have lots of fun with it "booing" at his friends and neighbors.

Thanksgiving

Thanksgiving holds very little historical significance for young children. They can, however, understand that it comes at the fall harvest time and that people are thoughtful and thankful to God for all the good things they have.

"We hope it means also a time of worship when the family attends church for a Thanksgiving service or when they have a special service of worship at home. We hope it means also a discovery that every day should be a day of thanks-giving and thanks-living."[1]

In the day-by-day living together in the group the teacher can make use of the normal experiences the children have with clothes, food, and love and care of their parents. She will help the children to understand that through their parents and the work of many people God cares for children. "She will lift these human and physical aspects to the higher level of having originally come from God, our Creator and the Provider of all that mankind needs."[2]

A part of the children's experiences centering around Thanksgiving will be in observing and enjoying the autumn season with all its lovely gifts. The children will delight in gathering colored leaves and seeds of all kinds. A big tray might be provided for exhibiting fall fruits and vegetables. After the children have enjoyed this collection for several days, they will find satisfaction in giving the food to someone who could use and enjoy it at Thanksgiving.

There are a number of books which teachers will find helpful as enrichment for the children at this special season of the year. Some of these are:

Claxton, Ernest, *A Child's Grace.* New York: E. P. Dutton & Co., Inc., 1948.
Jones, Elizabeth B., *God Loves Me.* Anderson, Ind.: Warner Press, 1954.
Jones, Elizabeth B., *Round About Me.* Anderson, Ind.: Warner Press, 1953.

Jones, Mary Alice, *Prayers and Graces for a Small Child.* Chicago: Rand McNally & Co., 1955.
Muller, Carolyn E., *God Planned It That Way.* New York: Abingdon-Cokesbury, 1952.
Van Meter, Harriett D., *Hands, Hands, Hands.* Richmond: John Knox Press, 1958.
White, Mary Sue, *I Know Why We Give Thanks.* Nashville: Broadman Press, 1956.
Wolcott, Carolyn Muller, *God Cares for Me.* New York: Abingdon Press, 1956.
Wolcott, Carolyn Muller, *God Gave Us Seasons.* New York: Abingdon Press, 1958.

The teacher will need to have available for the children magazines from which they can cut pictures of things for which they are thankful. A long strip of wrapping paper will be needed if the group is to make a frieze of the things for which they especially want to thank God. This frieze can be worked on from day to day as the children bring from home or find at school pictures which remind them of God's goodness in caring and providing for them.

Along with the frieze the group may create a litany of thanksgiving which will grow out of a feeling of real thankfulness. Psalm 75:1, Revised Standard Version, is a good verse to use in this way: "We give thanks to thee, O God."

The following litany is one which was created by a weekday church kindergarten group:

> For our homes and our mothers and daddies,
> "We give thanks to thee, O God."
> For our good food and warm clothes to wear,
> "We give thanks to thee, O God."
> For our kindergarten friends and the good times we have,
> "We give thanks to thee, O God."
> And for Jesus, who is the children's Friend,
> "We give thanks to thee, O God."
>
> Amen.

The following story is the kind that will help young children understand more fully ways in which God provides for our needs:

Giving Thanks

Psalms 104:24; 95:1; 1 Corinthians 3:9a

Johnny had just finished eating his dinner. "Thank you, Mother," he said, "for giving me that good baked apple for dessert."

"I'm glad that you liked it, Johnny," said his mother. "But I didn't give it to you. I just cooked it. Daddy bought the apples with the money that he earned."

"Well, then, I thank Daddy, too," said Johnny.

"But you know that Daddy had to buy them from the man at the store," said Mother.

"Then I thank the man at the store," said Johnny. "But where did he get the apple? This is a sort of game, isn't it?"

"Yes," said Mother. "A game of finding out how many people helped you get that baked apple. A man who drives a truck brought the apple to the store."

"Then I thank the truck driver, and the man who picked the apple off the tree," said Johnny. "And I guess that's all."

"Not quite all," said his mother. "We will have to thank the man who planted the apple tree, and the one who cares for it."

"Yes," said Johnny. "Is that all, now?"

"No," said Mother. "The most important one of all is God who sends the sun and the rain to make the apples grow, the one who makes the apple blossoms in the spring and the juicy red apples in the fall. You remember our Bible verse, don't you, Johnny? 'We give thanks to thee, O God.' Let's use it now as a thanksgiving prayer."

And Johnny repeated after his mother, "We give thanks to thee, O God."[3]

Thanksgiving holds significant spiritual values for young children when it is approached in a natural way on their level of comprehension and participation.

Teaching Aids

Denominational kindergarten curriculum materials with accompanying set of teaching pictures.

Songs: *Songs for Early Childhood*. Philadelphia: The Westminster Press, 1958.

Recordings: Geneva Records for the Children's Hour—for children 3, 4, and 5. Album: *Holidays*. Philadelphia: The Westminster Press, 1958. (One record is on Thanksgiving.)

Christmas

In the midst of the "hurry and flurry" and the "hustle and bustle" commonly attending the Christmas season, the young child is often placed in the position of becoming greatly overstimulated or of having to shift for himself as he "keeps out of mother's way while she's so busy." Add to this the one stock question, "What's Santa Claus going to bring you?" with which the child is repeatedly confronted, and then we begin to realize how difficult it is for the youngster to find the true meaning of Christmas.

During the weeks before Christmas, teachers of the weekday church group have the privilege and responsibility of helping the kindergarten children to develop more fully the Christian concept of Christmas. As they plan with the Sunday church leaders and the children's parents, they will find many opportunities for providing enriching experiences through which the children will realize that Christmas is the season when we celebrate the birthday of Jesus, who came to help us know and love God. Through these experiences they will grow in their understanding that we may show our love for Him by bringing happiness into the lives of other people. The children will find joy in such expressions of their gratitude, particularly at this season of the year.

The children's room should "speak" to them of the true spirit of the season. This will mean adequate preparation on the teacher's part in collecting Christmas pictures, books, and work materials, and in keeping the room organized for the best use of interest centers by the group.

The beauty spot should have a prominent place in the room as it displays a lovely Christmas picture (selected from the denominational kindergarten picture set), the Bible opened to the Christmas story, and a low vase of Christmas greens. During the last week of school the children will enjoy arranging and rearranging the figures of a crèche which might be placed on the small, low table with the open Bible.

The book table or bookshelves should display a number of good Christmas books for young children. The following have been found to be helpful and interesting to this age group:

Chalmers, Muriel, *The Star of the King*. New York: Thomas Nelson & Sons, 1947. Filmstrip in color is available by same title.
Chalmers, Muriel, *The Song the Shepherds Heard*. New York: Thomas Nelson & Sons, 1947. Filmstrip in color is available by same title.
Eberling, Georgia M., *When Jesus Was a Little Boy*. Chicago: Childrens Press, Inc., 1954.
Lloyd, Mary Edna, *Jesus, the Little New Baby*. Nashville: Abingdon Press, 1951.
Trent, Robbie, *A Star Shone*. Philadelphia: The Westminster Press, 1948.
Filmstrip series: "When Jesus Was Born." Kit No. 1, Family Filmstrips, Inc., "Jesus Is Born," "The Shepherds' Visit," "The Wise Men Bring Gifts."

Music

Music and Christmas just go together. Vocal and instrumental recordings of the best-loved Christmas carols will help to enrich the children's living during the days in which they are anticipating Christmas. The children will enjoy singing Christmas songs for weeks before Christmas. There are a number of songs which are more interesting with the accompaniment of rhythm instruments.

For example, bells and triangles go naturally with the song, "Ring, Ring, Ring the Bells," to the tune of "Row, Row, Row Your Boat."

> "Ring, ring, ring, the bells,
> Ring them loud and clear
> To tell to children everywhere
> That Christmas time is here."[4]

Bells and triangles also add reality to "Jingle Bells."

If arrangements can be made with the church organist, it will be well to plan for a visit to the church sanctuary one morning to enjoy organ music. The teacher should check beforehand with the organist regarding the children's favorite Christmas carols, particularly the ones they would enjoy singing with the organ accompaniment.

A good rhythmic activity during the pre-Christmas days would be dramatizing Santa's Toyshop at midnight when the toys are all supposed to dance and play and sing. Appropriate piano or recorded music may be played to accompany the activities of the various kinds of toys.

As the children work on the Christmas gifts they are making for their parents and friends, they will no doubt chant along in keeping with the work in which they are engaged. The children might create a melody for the following jingle to sing as a group occasionally while they work:

> We are Santa's helpers,
> Working hard today,
> Making gifts for others
> To have on Christmas Day.

Recordings

Christmas, from Geneva Records album on *Holidays.* Philadelphia: The Westminster Press, 1958.
Christmas Carols. Childcraft Records.
We Wish You a Merry Christmas. Greystone Corp., 100 Sixth Ave., New York 13, N. Y.
Christmas Hymns and Carols. Victor Chorus, directed by Robert Shaw.

Christmas Games

Hunt the Christmas Bell

Formation. Children seated informally on the floor.

Equipment. A small jingle bell fastened to a red paper bell.

Action. One child is chosen to hide with the bell while another child in the group is chosen to hide his eyes. When the child with the bell has found a place to hide, he rings the little bell. This is the signal for the other child to "wake up" and follow the sound of the tinkling bell until he finds where the child is hiding. When he discovers the child with the bell, two more children are chosen to take their places and the game starts over again.

Snowman and His Snowball (variation of Dog and Bone)

Formation. Children seated informally on the floor with a small chair out in front of the group.

Equipment. A snowball made of a large piece of cotton rolled into a ball and tied securely with white string.

Action. The snowman sits on the little chair with his back to the group and his eyes closed. His snowball is placed on the floor under his chair. A child is chosen from the group to try to retrieve the snowball without the snowman hearing him. If he is successful in getting back to his place with the snowball, and without the snowman hearing him, he becomes the next snowman. If not, he places the snowball back under the snowman's chair and another child is chosen to try to get it. The group may decide on a signal for the snowman to use if he hears the child getting away with his snowball. The child who returns to the group successfully will also need an appropriate signal.

Passing the Christmas Bell

Formation. Children seated on the floor in a circle.

Equipment. Red paper bell.

Action. One child is chosen to be "it" and sit in the center of the circle with his hands over his eyes. As the children sing the song, "We Are Passing the Christmas Bell," they pass the paper bell around the circle behind their backs. When the song ends, they all keep their hands behind them and the child in the center opens his eyes and tries to guess who has the bell.

Song. "We Are Passing the Christmas Bell"

Tune. "Here We Go 'Round the Mulberry Bush"

> We are passing a Christmas bell,
>   A Christmas bell, a Christmas bell,
> We are passing a Christmas bell,
>   Guess who has it now.

The children will delight in making the decorations for their kindergarten room and Christmas tree. This will mean having on hand a variety of scrap materials such as aluminum foil, colored cellophane, colored art paper, and all kinds of seed pods (magnolia pods, pine cones, sweet gum balls, catalpa beans, or whatever can be found in the local community). These may be painted with tempera paint and some of them sprinkled with "glitter" while the paint is still wet. In making the decorations, the children should be allowed to create without being hampered by patterns or "things" to color and cut out. Instead of the traditional popcorn stringing, which is too difficult for kindergarten children and likewise hazardous, the teacher may provide strips of aluminum foil and Scotch tape for simple chainmaking. The strips need to be ¾" x 5" for small children to use with ease in making the chain.

The children will enjoy making another simple chain to drape about over the tree. Large, colored paper drinking straws may be cut into lengths about 1¼" long. The children may string these on colored string tied to a short piece of plastic-covered copper wire which serves as a needle. The chain will be more interesting if small, odd-shaped pieces of colored paper are strung between the straws at intervals. The paper is more easily strung if it has a small hole punched in it (too small to allow the drinking straw to slip through).

Some groups may wish to make cookies of all shapes to tie about over the tree. If the teacher does not want to keep "temptation" before the children in this way, she may provide a salt-dough mixture, a rolling pin, and small cookie cutters of animals, bells, stars, and other interesting shapes. Food coloring may be added to the mixture of one cup of flour and one cup of salt to which is added enough water to render a texture like bread dough. A hole should be punched in each ornament before it dries so that a ribbon or string may be inserted for hanging on the tree. When dried at room temperature, the salt will give the ornaments a dainty sparkle.

The tree, when decorated, may be far from meeting an adult's standard of beauty, but it will be the joy and delight of the children who helped to create it.

Making gifts for their parents can be a very happy and satisfying experience if the children are allowed to make gifts which they can create without having to conform to a pattern or necessitating adult help.

Several Christmas paintings, created especially for their parents, might be rolled up and tied with red ribbon. This makes a most acceptable gift. It might be well, in a parents' newsletter, to warn the mothers and daddies of the arrival of the "gift" in order that they may be prepared to refrain from questioning and to display surprise and appreciation appropriately.

In sections of the country where the wild birds need supplementary feeding during the winter months, the children will enjoy decorating a Christmas tree for the birds. A bare branch of a tree may be sunk into a large can or bucket of dirt. The children can tie pieces of suet and wedges of apple on the branches. The tree may be set outside the kindergarten windows where the children can watch the birds feeding.

Well-selected Christmas stories and poems play a big part in helping to build feelings and attitudes. The Christmas story from the second chapter of Luke should be used frequently and in different ways. The teacher will first tell the story from the Bible, and then she may use pictures and let the children tell the story. The colored filmstrips, "The Song the Shepherds Heard," "The Star of the King," or "When Jesus Was Born" may be used at other times with the five-year-olds. They will enjoy dramatizing the story, too. Just a square scarf and a sash are all the costuming necessary to help the children get into the spirit of the shepherds' visit to see the Christ Child.

Keeping the parents informed from time to time of the current activities in which their child is participating not only helps them to better interpret the weekday church program, but also suggests types of activities which they might provide for their child in his home. A December news bulletin could serve as a medium of communicating information to the child's home regarding the purposes of the Christmas unit as developed for the weekday church kindergarten and the activities planned to realize these purposes in the lives of the children.

Planning a party to honor their parents and younger brothers and sisters is always a joyous experience for all concerned. There is *no planned program,* but rather just a time when the parents come to share with the children a part of their school's Christmas activities. As they sit around the Christmas tree, everyone joins in singing a number of the Christmas songs. The party would not be complete without the Bible story from Luke 2. It could be shared with the parents in any way the group chooses.

Because the children are usually already overstimulated in their homes in the anticipation of Christmas, it is wise to keep the Christmas party of short duration and as simple as possible.

During the Christmas season the teachers will be especially aware of the children's need for a relaxed, unhurried atmosphere in which to work and play in the group. They will want to provide the children with ample time and opportunities for making free choices, participating in group planning, and finding joy in the simple, happy experiences of getting ready for Christmas with their friends at the weekday school.

Valentine's Day

Valentine's Day is a very special time for young children. It is a time of thinking of friends—a time for children to enjoy among themselves. It is a time of making and receiving happy surprises. It offers further opportunity for the children to experiment with paper, paste, and scissors, crayons and paints, seals, paper doilies, and scraps of "this and that"—colored paper, drinking straws, scraps from sample wallpaper books, small artificial flowers from discarded dress ornaments, small feathers, and bits of ribbon and lace and cloth of heavy texture.

Most five-year-olds find it easy to cut paper hearts bilaterally. They can learn this skill by using newspaper until they learn to cut away from the fold.

Children enjoy bringing the commercial-type Valentine from home for their friends. They should not be discouraged in doing so, but should be encouraged to *make* Valentines for their friends. "No commercial Valentines . . . can possibly substitute for the products of the children's own heads and hands, which involve experimentation, sense experience, judgment, responsibility, and the joy of creation."[5]

A Valentine box is not satisfactory for young children. It is hard for them to wait patiently as the Valentines are distributed. But worse still, distributing the Valentines from the box allows everyone to see "how many" the other children receive. This can be bad for the popular child as well as for the timid little fellow who doesn't seem to have many friends, as indicated by the few Valentines he receives.

Some teachers find that having a Valentine "Post Office" is a much easier way to handle the distribution. Each child brings an adult-size shoe box to school the first of February. He may paint it and decorate it if he chooses. The teacher will cut one end of the box about $2\frac{1}{2}$ inches deep and the full width of the box. When the lid is placed back on the box there will be a slot left for posting Valentines. Each box will have the child's name below the slot. The older children will enjoy trying to match the names and mail their own Valentines. The day before Valentine's Day the teacher can check quickly and be certain that the Valentines are all in the correct boxes. She can also have on hand some "extras" in case some of the children were not well remembered. Then, at the appointed time on the day of the celebration each child receives his box of Valentines to open and enjoy. Each one is so busy with his own Valentines that he isn't as apt to be aware of any differences in numbers received. One other good feature about this method is that each child has his box in which he can take his Valentines home. He is spared the heartache of losing them or of getting them mixed up with other children's Valentines.

Valentine songs, poems, and stories used for days before Valentine's Day make it really a "Valentine Season" for the children. Perhaps a simple party will be planned for the day of the celebration. Decorations for the table and decorations on the napkins can both be planned and executed by the children days ahead of February 14. Heart-shaped cookies and red punch will delight the children and give a real party touch to the day's celebration.

The children will enjoy playing simple games which have a Valentine flavor. Several of the games played at Halloween time can be adapted for Valentine time.

As in all celebrations with young children, care needs to be taken to keep the activities simple and spread out over long enough time to avoid the hustle and bustle that make for overstimulation in the children.

Easter Time

Easter time is a joyous season for young and old alike. Nursery and kindergarten children cannot comprehend the deep significance of its meaning, but they can catch the spirit of rejoicing and appreciate the newness of life manifested in the natural world about them.

They thrill again and again over the bursting buds, the flowers that "appear on the earth," and the soft, new green grass. They can remember that only a short while before, the trees and shrubs were bare and the grass looked dead. They recall the little brown bulbs which they planted (wondering what could possibly happen to them), and find that now they have beautiful white flowers growing from them. At this season there are many occasions for the child's experiencing wonder and awe—moments of real worship for him and his group.

Weekday church groups will celebrate Easter, but in ways that differ from their celebrations of the other special days or seasons of the year. Some of the parents may suggest giving an Easter party or egg hunt. Such activities do not seem to be in keeping with the spiritual tone of this special season. If for no other reason an Easter egg hunt is inappropriate for young children because it involves keen competition in hunting for the eggs. The shy, timid, or less mature children—who do not need to experience failure—are usually left behind without discovering any eggs, while the aggressive children bolt forth and make the find. Even dividing the eggs equally among the children after the hunt does not ease the pain of the disappointment and frustration experienced by the unsuccessful children.

Celebrating the Easter season with young children in the weekday group should embody a spiritual emphasis. On Palm Sunday the children will probably have had the story of the triumphal entry with special recognition of the part the children played in honoring Jesus. This story can be recalled during the week.

The teachers will want to be alert to questions the children may raise regarding events of Passion Week. Questions are likely to come because young children often hear discussions in the home, see television pre-Easter programs, or have some experience with pictures portraying the death of Jesus. This is also a very natural time for young children to bring up their questions about death.

The teachers will want to be prepared themselves so that they can recognize any contribution the children may make about the crucifixion without dwelling on details which would be in any way disturbing to the group. They will want to answer the children's questions honestly and directly and with Biblical accurateness. The weekday teachers will need to keep well in mind the teaching materials which will be used for Easter in the Sunday church kindergarten. They will want to exercise care that they do not take the edge off the teaching plans for the Sunday session. This will mean that the teachers of the Sunday and weekday groups will want to plan and work very carefully together that the Easter experience of the children will be satisfying and an altogether joyous one.

One very helpful approach to Easter for young children is remembering the stories of Jesus with which they are familiar. This will mean recalling some of His teachings and the things He did for people as He "went about doing good."

The children will need to be helped to think of Easter as a time of sharing their happiness with others. They will enjoy making simple Easter cards for their friends at the church. They might know of a shut-in person living near the church who would enjoy some special attention at this time. The children could plan ways of sharing good things with this friend.

They might bake cookies and pack a small box as a gift. They might want to share their bowl of flowers which they had planted and cared for and enjoyed. Some of the children might suggest painting spring pictures as another gift to take. They could plan to sing several of their best-loved springtime songs and songs of praise. This experience could be one of deep spiritual significance for the children.

Adequate planning for such a project will involve making advance arrangements with the family in the home to be visited and getting written permission from the parents for the children to leave the church grounds.

Each of these experiences at the young child's present stage of maturity is helping to lay a sound basis for an expanding concept of Easter in all its fullness of meaning for the growing Christian. In this approach, the child has a satisfying experience of Easter and will have nothing to unlearn as he grows and matures in the faith.

Birthdays

Birthdays are very important to the young child. They symbolize "growing up" and "bigger" for him. On his fourth birthday Danny held up four fingers and proudly announced, "Today I am this many. Next year I'll be a whole handful."

One reason a birthday is so special is that it belongs to no one else. It is the child's own day—the day when he is given special attention. In the weekday group the day centers around and honors him. He may choose his favorite story or music when the group is together. He will have the honor of some extra responsibility in the group because he is "older now." There will be a birthday song or two and a prayer for him, also. This can be a most meaningful experience for the entire group.

Children often create birthday "surprises" for one another during their work and play time. It may be a birthday card or a special picture painted in gay colors. Mary had a delightful time painting a birthday picture for her friend Janice and then surprising her with it later in the morning. In the center of the picture was a large cake "iced" in red, with five red candles arranged carefully on top. Around the cake were five birthday presents, each painted a different color. What joy this experience did bring to both little girls!

The child's birthday may be indicated on the calendar with a small picture of a birthday cake pasted on the date. He will enjoy watching to see the days go by as shown on the calendar. The child approaching five or six may want to count the days until his birthday.

Simplicity is the keynote of the child's birthday celebration at school. However, it is a day filled with warmth and good will sincerely expressed in a number of ways by his kindergarten friends. His birthday celebration at school often means more to the child than the elaborate party given him at home.

The nursery school teacher will recognize that much of the foregoing discussion about celebrating special days applies particularly to the kindergarten. Such activities for the three-year-olds will be much more simplified. The nursery teacher will need to adapt and plan for the kinds of experiences which best meet the needs and interests of her group for the special days of the year.

Chapter VI

The Program for
Young Children (Part I)

Experiencing Music Together with Young Children

"There is nothing more constant in the life of the young child than sound and movement. Consequently, there is no time in which music is so integrated with life as in the early years."[1]

With ease and naturalness music can flow in and out of the day's program through such experiences as singing, listening, and rhythmic activities. Emphasis is on the *joy* which the music experiences realize for the young child; performance and the achievement of perfection are never the aim with this age.

Singing

Singing is essentially an activity for fun and satisfaction. The teacher, keeping this in mind as well as the developmental level of the young child with regard to music, will not expect too much of him. She will accept what the child is able to do, and will help him to raise his own standard of achievement in ways that will enhance his love for music.

Singing activities should be spontaneous as well as planned, and may occur almost any time during the session. If there is a scheduled time for singing activities, care needs to be taken that it does not immediately follow a time of vigorous activity.

A happy, relaxed atmosphere is essential if children are to participate joyously, find release from tensions, and grow in their ability to sing and to find satisfaction in a variety of music experiences.

When children feel free and comfortable, they will spontaneously burst into song or chant as they work and play. One might hear Ted as he pushes his block train over the floor chanting, "Toot, toot, here I come, Toot, toot, here I come. Toot, toot, toot." Or from the home center it might be Susan singing softly to her doll who is almost asleep, "Close your eyes, sleepy baby. Close your eyes, sleep, sleep. Close your eyes, sleepy baby. Sleep, baby, sleep." And at one of the easels, Keith as he paints a lovely rain picture may be heard

Dramatic play: Barn and adjoining pen are made with large blocks.

Dramatic play: A mother makes purchases at the corner grocery.

A visit to hear the church organ enriches appreciation of music.

A father visits the school and shares the children's activities.

singing to the rhythm of his paintbrush, "The rain is splishing, splashing, splashing, splashing. The rain is coming down, coming down. Splash!"

Occasionally, the teacher might record the children's spontaneous songs and use them with the group at some later time. Original songs, like the children's own stories, often have more appeal than the "ready-made" songs in the music books. Such was the case in a kindergarten in which the children asked to sing one of their musical creations every day for many days, even on the brightest and sunniest of days. Their song, which had grown out of a group experience of listening to and watching the rain, was more than just a song. It was the culmination of a happy time with science observations and language development mixed together with melody and rhythm.

RAIN

Kindergarten, 1958   A. T. S. Kindergarten, 1958

"Pit - ter, Pat - ter," says the rain   As   it hits our win-dow-pane.
Lit - tle   riv - ers made   of rain Run-ning down our win-dow-pane.

"It is important that these beginnings of music making should focus on the constant encouragement of this way of expressing himself and not on the product itself. . . . What is important is not the preservation of any special song that a child creates, but the preservation of a way of life that will keep on inspiring him to experiment freely."[2]

Conversational singing has special appeal for young children. Sometimes the teacher can save a child or a group from a tense situation by singing lightly her counsel or brief comments. A musical warning that free playtime is almost over is often more easily accepted by the children than other methods which might be used. To the tune of "London Bridge Is Falling Down" the teacher might sing quietly as she moves about the room from group to group:

> Clean-up time is almost here,
> Almost here, almost here;
> Clean-up time is almost here;
> We'll be ready.

With a little ingenuity the teacher can improvise a number of such chants. And even clean-up time can become glamorous if it has a musical setting. The following song to the tune of "The Farmer in the Dell" is an effective way of bringing playtime to a close gracefully and of enlisting workers for the clean-up detail:

> Good helpers we will be,
> Good helpers we will be,
> There's work for all, there's work for all.
> Good helpers we will be.

> or

> We're cleaning up our room,
> We're cleaning up our room,
> We're putting all our toys away,
> We're cleaning up our room.

Another chant to the tune of the chorus of the singing game "Pawpaw Patch" could go something like this:

> We're picking up our toys and
>   putting them away;
> We're picking up our toys and
>   putting them away;
> We're picking up our toys and
>   putting them away;
> We're putting our toys away.

As with all techniques, this method would grow ineffective with overuse.

Selecting Songs

In selecting songs the first consideration is given to the range of notes, which should fall generally between middle C and D above high C. To evaluate the general fitness of a song before selecting it for use with young children, the following criteria need to be applied:

1. The song should be truly artistic.
2. It should be short and simple.
3. It should embody a definite and unchanging rhythm, with some repetition of phrases.
4. It should carry one main idea.
5. It should relate to the child's experiences.

Teaching a New Song

When the song which is to be taught is in keeping with the immediate interest of the group, there is little need to talk about it. Often introductory discussions detract from the song itself. The new song should be sung to the children from beginning to end without accompaniment. It should be sung correctly, distinctly, and interestingly so that the children hear the right melody and words. The children will usually respond with a "Sing it again." Then they will attempt to sing along with the teacher. The teacher's own voice is the most effective way of ensuring that the children sing in a light, relaxed manner. To avoid voice strain the teacher may need to suggest that they use their "light, happy voices" as they sing.

The phrase-by-phrase, rote method of teaching songs has no appeal to the young child. He learns more easily if he sings the song as a whole. And he should learn the words and the melody together.

Much of young children's singing should be done without the accompaniment of the piano. It is easier for the children to match the teacher's voice than an instrument; then, too, they are apt to become too dependent upon the instrument. After the children have become quite familiar with the melody, they will profit from and enjoy singing with the piano. Occasional use of other instruments to accompany the children in their singing sparks their interest and enriches their music experiences greatly. The autoharp, xylophone, or resonator bells are good instruments to use in this way.

Teacher's Personal Collection of Songs

The teacher may have a number of the recommended songbooks for young children, but she will want her own collection, too. From time to time new songs are printed in the church school kindergarten curriculum materials. When these songs fill a need for the weekday group, the teacher should clip them and add to her collection. A large loose-leaf notebook which will lie flat against the piano is the most usable type of book. Manila tag filing folders, cut and punched to fit the notebook, make durable pages on which to paste the songs. The group will enjoy the book if pictures illustrating the song are included. This can be a very helpful teaching tool which can "grow" from year to year.

Singing Games

When we observe a group of young children playing "Fly, Little Blue Bird," "Looby Loo," "Round and Round the Village," or any other simple singing game, we can be sure that a majority of the children are participating. Timid children who do not usually sing with the group at other times will become absorbed in the game, lose themselves in it, and sing.

Care should be taken that the children who are engaged in the active part of a game should not try to sing, also. There are good recordings of a number of the simpler singing games. These may be used to vary the children's experiences with this kind of music activity.

Singing games may be found in a number of songbooks for use in early childhood education. The following are a few singing games which teachers have found popular with the younger set:

"The Farmer in the Dell," "Looby Loo," "Round and Round the Village," "Punchinello," "Fly, Little Blue Bird," "Here We Go 'Round the Mulberry Bush," "London Bridge," and "Did You Ever See a Lassie?"

Listening Activities

Listening is a very important part of the weekday music program. Some time should be provided each day for quiet listening. This may be enjoying a short instrumental or vocal recording by a few children, or it may be listening to quiet music for the entire group during the rest time.

Listening activities may involve quietly enjoying recorded music on the record player or instrumental music played by parents or friends of the children. A trip to the church sanctuary to enjoy organ music can be a most rewarding experience for young children and their teachers.

Listening activities not only provide pleasure but also help to develop auditory discrimination. As the group listens to music, the children will have opportunities for recognizing familiar melodies, determining whether the music is sad or happy, slow or fast, loud or soft. Listening to music also serves to stimulate the children's imagination. As they listen for "pictures" or stories in the music, they give thought to it and sometimes respond with interpretations through bodily movement. But above all, listening to fine music develops deep within the children a real love and appreciation for fine music.

The teacher will also take advantage of every opportunity for helping the children become aware of nature's music—the melody of the wind in the trees, the rhythm of raindrops, the noises of insects, and the songs of birds.

Rhythms

Through rhythmic activities the child develops muscular co-ordination, balance, poise, and good posture. He finds release from tensions and an outlet for dramatic urges. He learns to listen and to interpret meanings through bodily responses, and he develops skills and control in the use of his body.

The child develops his rhythmic awareness through experiences with a variety of accompaniments. For the young child the piano seems best, because the teacher can adapt the tempo of the accompaniment to fit the child's tempo. The teacher needs to watch closely as the child walks, runs, or gallops, and to follow him with the appropriate music. As the child matures in his control and technique of movement, he can begin to follow and interpret.

Percussion instruments, particularly drums, make good accompaniment for rhythmic expression. The children themselves can create rhythmic patterns on the drum to accompany the movements of other children.

The most difficult accompaniment for the young child is the recording. Here the tempo is fixed. However, when the children have matured enough to listen to the recorded music and hear it with their whole bodies, and when they are free to express their own rhythmic feelings, they usually respond to the music quite freely and with varied expressions.

Such materials as large squares of thin cloth or silk scarves, long turkey feathers, wooden hoops, help children to extend themselves into space with freer bodily movements. These "props" aid in stimulating imagination and help children who are conscious of their hands to find ways of using them to help them dance.

Many of the simple songs which children in the kindergarten enjoy singing suggest some fundamental rhythmic movement or creative rhythmic play-acting. The following are typical examples of this kind of accompaniment:

Walking Down the Street

> "(Use child's name) goes a-walking
> Down the street, down the street, down the street;
> _____ goes a-walking down the street,
> How are you to-day?
> _____ comes a-knocking
> At your door, at your door, at your door;
> _____ comes a-knocking at your door,
> Come outside and play."[3]

Interpretation. The child chosen walks around the room as the group sings the first stanza. On the second stanza, he taps lightly on another child's shoulder, who in turn becomes "It." (Words for the action may be changed as the group desires, to hopping, trotting, skipping, or other rhythms.) To vary the method and include all the children, each child when chosen becomes a partner. Then he in turn chooses a child to be his partner. Each of the partners then chooses a new partner until everyone in the group is participating with a partner.

Guessing Game

> "Ding, dong, ding, dong,
> Ding, dong bell,
> What has this man to sell?
>
> "Ding, dong, ding, dong,
> Ding, dong bell,
> What can it be?"[4]

Interpretation. The child chosen as the peddler walks around the room ringing a bell and when the group sings, "What can it be?", he calls out his wares.

Using Musical Instruments

Young children need a variety of instruments with which to experiment—drums of different sizes, triangles, cymbals, tambourines, tone blocks, and resonator bells.

Having the instruments does not mean that there should be a rhythm band "so that the children can learn to keep time to music." When the teacher "trains" young children to function together in a rhythm band, she is making it hard for them ever to use the instruments creatively. It does for them what "coloring in" a hectographed picture does—it stifles their imagination and imposes adult standards upon them. This experience also hurts the shy youngsters and those whose rhythmic responses are less pronounced. These children never have the opportunity to enjoy using the more distinctive rhythm instruments because they might ruin the quality of the performance of the group. Then, too, it is usually the child in the group who exhibits the keenest sense of rhythm who is always chosen to be the leader. Hours of "practicing" usually precede each performance, even to the point of fatigue on the part of the children. Then comes the "show" with the youngsters dressed in their band costumes and keyed up to a high emotional pitch. And fond parents, basking in the glory of their offspring, are certain that theirs is surely a budding musical genius.

Mrs. Emma Sheehy has this observation regarding rhythm band experiences for young children:

"Yes, it is possible to train any group of little children to keep time, and they will accept a plan laid down from above. Whether or not it is sound procedure from the standpoint of child development and of musical development is another question. Certainly the value of a rhythm band in training children to keep time to music can be discounted. If children have plenty of opportunity to use their bodies in a free and rhythmic way, if they have frequent use of instruments individually and in small groups, and—above all—if they are relaxed and free of tension, then keeping time is something we need not train them to do. We can't keep them from doing it! It is as natural to them as running and jumping!

"The instruments generally used in a rhythm band can be used by children in a creative way, as and when the need for them is evident."[5] For example, a child recognizing the similarity of the sound of the tone block to the galloping hoofs of horses will ask to play the tone block while the group sings about the galloping ponies. Tambourines add color to some creative dancing, and drums add to children's fun when they are toy soldiers marching around the room. Children almost always ask to use the triangles for the song, "Twinkle, Twinkle, Little Star." They will choose rhythm sticks to represent the ticking of a clock as in the song, "Hickory, Dickory, Dock." And what could be better than the clash of a cymbal for the one o'clock striking of the clock, and running the mallet down the scale on the xylophone for the little mouse's quick retreat down the clock? Sandpaper blocks add reality to an imaginary train, and certain rhythms, when beat out on a drum, will stimulate a transformation of the group. There before one's very eyes, as if by magic, young Indians suddenly appear in a tribal dance.

Creating tunes or picking out familiar tunes on resonator bells, a small marimba, or tuned bottles are all good experiences in experimentation for the young child.

Homemade Instruments

Although it is better for young children to have musical instruments of finest quality, it is also good to experiment with sound from homemade instruments.

Horseshoes that are free from rust give much the same effect as the triangle. The horseshoe will need to be suspended by a cord (as in the case of the triangle) to produce the best quality of tone.

Sandblocks, two blocks of wood 3″ x 4″ x 2″ with coarse sandpaper tacked over one side, make very satisfactory swishing sounds when rubbed together.

Rhythm sticks may be made of twelve-inch lengths of ¾ inch dowels. Old broom handles may be used, being sure to keep the sticks from the same broom together as a pair. The wood in broom handles is often more resonant than that of doweling.

Tuned bottles are interesting for the group to make and use for tapping out familar tunes or creating original ones. Quart fruit-juice bottles, or large medicine bottles which can be obtained from a pharmacy, are satisfactory. Eight bottles of the same size and kind are necessary for an octave. A good deal of experimentation is necessary to discover just the right amounts of water to use in each bottle to produce the right tone. If the bottles are clear glass they will be more attractive and interesting if a different color is added to each bottle. Food coloring or tempera paint may be used but should be added before the tuning has been completed. Capping the bottles will keep them as originally tuned. When the bottles are uncapped, the water evaporates and thus changes the tone of the bottles.

Drums of varying sizes may be made from barrels, kegs, small wooden buckets, or fiber drums with metal rims. Fiber drums may be secured from institutions such as hotels, hospitals, or schools purchasing detergent in 50 and 100 pound drums. Those which have the lock-on metal rims hold the drumhead more securely. The drumheads may be made of used skin drumheads, which may be obtained reasonably at music equipment houses. New drumheads may be purchased but are rather expensive.

One of the easiest and most practical drums can be made with any kind of keg, barrel, or fiber drum and a special cloth for the drumhead. (This is not an activity for the child but can be a co-operative enterprise for parents and children. The parents can construct the drum and let the children do the painting necessary to make a finished product.)

The drumhead is made from cloth—a very close-woven ticking sometimes called "Gold Cloth" and sometimes called "Bohemian ticking." The head is cut to hang about three inches over the barrel. The glossy side of the cloth is turned to the inside of the drum. Strong cord is wound around the cloth several times near the top of the drum and is tied securely. Then the cloth is stretched as tightly as possible, requiring two persons pulling on opposite sides of the drum and tacking the cloth along every few inches. If there is a metal rim which locks, it can then be put in place and locked. The extra cloth which comes down below the rim may be covered with wide plastic tape or "contact" paper available in dime stores. The head has to have two or three coats of a mixture of three parts clear airplane dope and one part lacquer thinner. After the head is painted, the drum itself may be painted. Tempera paint is quite satisfactory and is easy for children to use.

Drumsticks may be made by using the largest round fishing cork available and pushing into it a dowel stick which is the size of the hole in the cork. The cork may be painted with tempera paint and then covered with a coat of clear shellac. The drum is ready then to provide fun for all, indoors and out.

The Teacher's Role

To ensure good rhythmic experiences, the teacher provides a happy, permissive atmosphere, plenty of room, rich firsthand experiences, and good rhythmic accompaniment.

The thoughtful teacher makes use of space and equipment indoors and out in such a way that the group is encouraged to experiment with sound and rhythmic movement in experiences which are satisfactory to them.

The teacher enriches the children's experiences by being able to draw upon a wide repertoire of songs and by creating spontaneously when needs arise in the group.

The teacher always keeps in mind the fact that she is not attempting to make musicians of the children. She is concerned not so much with what they can do musically as with how the music experiences contribute to the growth and development of the individual children.

She will allow for creativity to flow through every type of musical activity. "The teacher must never allow herself to be held back by lack of formal music training. Her attitude is more important than her skill. Actually, the opportunity for the resourceful teacher to join with the children on their level, unhampered by rigid traditions or preconceived methods, might prove to the youngsters that music is a dynamic experience in which one can explore and experiment *ad infinitum*. Enthusiasm is contagious. Children will quickly sense the genuine interest of their teacher and share it."[6]

Music Bibliography

Association for Childhood Education International, *Music for Children's Living*. Washington, D. C.: A. C. E. I., 1955.

Andrews, Gladys, *Creative Rhythmic Movement for Children*. Englewood Cliffs: Prentice-Hall, Inc., 1954.

Heffernan, Helen, editor, California Supervisors Association, *Guiding the Young Child*. Boston: D. C. Heath & Company, 1959.

California State Department of Education, *Teachers Guide to Education in Early Childhood*. Sacramento: California State Department of Education, 1956. Chapter 12.

Children and Records. Children's Work Section, National Council of Churches, 1955.

Jones, Betty J., *What Is Music for Young Children?* National Association for Nursery Education. Distribution Center—University of Rhode Island, Kingston, R. I.

Music Educators' National Conference, *Music for Early Childhood*. Information Leaflet. Source Material Listings: Books and Record Companies. Edited by Adeline McCall. M. E. N. E., 643 Jackson Blvd., Chicago, Ill.

Roorbach, Rosemary, *Using Records with Young Children*. Leaflet. National Council of the Churches of Christ in the U. S. A.

Sheehy, Emma D., *There's Music in Children*. New York: Henry Holt & Co., Inc., 1952.

Shields, Elizabeth McE., *Music in the Religious Growth of Children*. New York: Abingdon Press, 1943.

Songbooks

Crowninshield, Ethel, *The Sing and Play Book*. Boston: Boston Music Co., 1948.

Crowninshield, Ethel, *Stories that Sing*. Boston: Boston Music Co., 1945.

Landeck, Beatrice, *Songs to Grow On*. New York: William Sloane Associates, 1952. Record album of selected songs from this book made by Folkways Record and Service Corporation, 117 W. 46th St., New York, N. Y.

McConathy, *et al.*, *Music for Early Childhood* from *New Music Horizons Series*. New York: Silver Burdett Co., 1952. Album of recordings of many of the songs of the song book.

Pitts, Glenn, and Waters, *The Kindergarten Book* from *Our Singing World Series*. New York: Ginn & Company, 1949. Album K of selected songs from the song book.
Songs of Early Childhood for Church and Home. Philadelphia: The Westminster Press, 1958.
Lloyd, Mary Edna, *We Sing Together*. Graded Press, 1958.
Thomas, Edith L., *Martin and Judy Songs*. Boston: Beacon Press, 1948.
Wessells, Katherine T., *The Golden Song Book*. New York: Simon and Schuster, Inc., 1954.
Wessells, Katherine T., *The Little Golden Book of Singing Games*. New York: Simon and Schuster, Inc., 1947.

Record Sources

American Teaching Aids Co. publishes a consolidated catalog of resources. 102 Elizabeth Avenue, Hempstead, N. Y.
Greystone Corp., 100 Sixth Avenue, New York, N. Y. publishes the Curriculum Guide which suggests ways of using their records. They produce records with the following labels:
    Pram, ages 1 and 2
    Young Peoples' Records, Ages 2-5; 6-10
    Children's Record Guild, Ages 2-4; 5-8
Childhood Rhythms; Series I. Arranged by Ruth Evans, Box 132, P. O. Branch, Springfield, Mass.

Creative Art Experiences for Young Children

One of the important daily responsibilities of the teacher is to provide for the children an environment conducive to satisfying, happy art experiences. This will not necessitate an expensive outlay of equipment and materials, but it will mean having the right kinds and sizes of art equipment and supplies in readiness for the children's use when they need them. Having the materials prepared and arranged in the art area of the room before the children arrive is the best way to interest them in participating in art activities. In a well-organized room where the work materials are accessible to the children we can almost hear the paint, clay, chalk, crayons, and paper calling out to the children as they enter the room, "Come try me and see what you can do and say with me."

Painting

Some teachers prefer the use of tables to easels for the children's painting. The child, as he stands at the table, has better control over the brush; he can make large, free, swinging strokes on the paper. Then, too, as the child paints at the table or on the floor, he is not so apt to have the experience of paint running down his picture as when he paints at an easel. However, when space will allow, it is well to have one or two double easels so that the child may have the experience of painting at an easel. He can then choose the method he prefers for his painting.

Materials needed for providing good painting experiences:

Paint. Powdered tempera in red, yellow, blue, green, brown, orange, magenta, black, and white should be available. It is less expensive to buy the one-pound cans of dry tempera and mix as needed than to buy the ready-mixed show-card paint. The best results in preparing this opaque paint for use may be obtained in the following way:

a. Pour into small container the amount of water desired.

b. Pour the powdered paint into the water slowly, mixing thoroughly to a thin, creamy consistency. When the paint will cover the print of newspaper, it is thick enough for use.

Paint extender. Liquid starch may be added to tempera paint to improve the texture and eliminate some of the dripping—about two tablespoons of starch to each small container of paint. Another mixture may be made and used in the same amounts as a paint extender by cooking cornstarch to the consistency of gravy. It should be cooked in a double boiler.

Paper for painting. Unprinted newsprint, 18″ x 24″, is usually the least expensive paper to use for painting. It is easy for the child to use because it is so absorbent. The classified ad section of the daily news is quite satisfactory for painting pictures, particularly if the paint is mixed to the right consistency.

Brushes. These should be large, long-handled, black-bristle brushes, preferably flat, sizes ½″ and ¾″ and 1″ in width. There should be enough on hand so that there will be a brush for each container of paint. Nursery children will probably have a better experience with the ¾″ and 1″ brushes, while the older child will be able to use the ½″ brush with satisfaction.

Half-pint waxed paper milk cartons. These make excellent containers for the mixed paint. This eliminates the danger of accidents from broken paint jars. If tin or plastic containers are used for paint "jars," they must be thoroughly cleaned before mixing fresh paint in

them. When the paint containers are covered tightly the paint
has a tendency to sour, especially black paint.

Empty #10 food cans. Large cans are excellent to have on the
table ready for the children to use for washing their brushes. Be certain that the top has been smoothly cut out.

Smocks. These can be very easily made from men's discarded sport
shirts. Buttoned down the back, the shirt covers the child well and
at the same time allows freedom of movement. Smocks are necessary
equipment for most art activities. If the shirts are too large for the
children, they may be made to fit by taking a tuck over each shoulder
until the sleeve is raised to a place comfortable for the child.

Finger Painting

A formica-top table, counter top, or large pieces of white oilcloth
will be needed for this activity.

The finger paint may be purchased in liquid or powder form or
may be made, using the following recipe:

> ⅝ cup of laundry starch
> 1 pint of water
> ¾ cup soap flakes
> ¼ cup talcum powder
> 1 teaspoon oil of cloves or
> oil of sassafras to preserve
> the mixture, keeping it
> from souring.

Mix the starch with a little cold water to make a creamy paste.
Add to pint of water and cook slowly until mixture becomes "clear"
or glossy. Stir constantly. Let the mixture cool a bit, then add soap
flakes, stirring until evenly distributed. Add oil of sassafras. (Note:
if the starch mixture becomes too stiff as it cooks, thin with a little
water. Avoid letting it become lumpy.) Color may be added in the
jar, mixing in the dry tempera. However, children enjoy adding
the color themselves. This can be done if the powdered tempera is
put into salt shakers. After the child has spread the clear starch
mixture all over the surface he is to paint, he may sprinkle on the
desired color and work it about over the paper until it is thoroughly
mixed.

Finger paint paper is ideal for making finger paint "pictures," but because of the cost involved, many schools have turned to a less expensive paper. Roll shelf paper which is glazed on one side serves the purpose quite well. The widest roll, preferably 18″, should be used. Pieces can be cut 24″ long. The 18″ x 24″ size will allow the child opportunity for large, sweeping movements over the paper.

A large sponge may be used to thoroughly wet the glazed side of the paper. The child is then ready to spread two tablespoonfuls of the paint all over the paper with the palm of his hand. (If the dry tempera is to be added, the mixture is now ready.) What happens next on the paper is a surprise to everyone as the child moves his hand, fingers, fingernails, and fist or arm about through the paint. The child's "picture" may be saved by lifting it carefully by the bottom corners and laying it out on newspaper to dry. The newspaper absorbs the moisture from the paper, aiding in the drying of the paint. If the paper curls on the edges when dry, it may be pressed on the unpainted side with a warm iron.

Finger painting done right on a formica-top table without paper, however, gives the child complete freedom and lessens attempts at trying to "draw a picture" with the use of his index finger. The younger child has a much better experience if he uses the finger paint without the paper. He will experiment with the medium more readily and use more freely both his whole hands, his arms, and even his elbows. Every movement the child makes in the paint is a creation of design and rhythm. The child's "creation" may be preserved for him by placing a sheet of newsprint (12″ x 18″) on top of his finger painting and smoothing it down carefully. When lifted, this paper will have a print of the finger painting.

As a medium, finger paint or hand paint as it might be called, frees the child to give vent to his feelings and to find release from tensions. He can achieve a variety of effects with the paint as he tries the palm of his hand, his knuckles, the side of his hand, his fist, and fingernails. Discovering these effects and the effects of mixing colors, and exploring different techniques in controlling the paint, are a part of the pleasure and satisfaction the child derives from finger painting.

Clay Modeling

Moist potter's clay is preferable for use by young children. If it is not available locally as a natural resource, powdered clay may be purchased from an art or school supply house. Directions for mixing are given on the package. The ready-mixed clay is also available in five-pound packages but is more expensive.

A ten-gallon galvanized garbage pail with a tightly fitting lid can be used for storing the clay to keep it moist and in good condition for modeling. A damp cloth kept over the clay will also help, especially if the clay is kept in large balls ready for the children to use. The clay may be kept in small plastic bags and then stored in the galvanized can. Each time the clay is put away it should be rolled into balls the size of a baseball. A hole should be punched in each ball and the hole filled with water. The clay should be squeezed together over the hole before being stored. Hardened clay which has not been baked may be reclaimed for use by breaking it up and pouring water over it slowly until all the water is absorbed. It is usually necessary to let this clay stand for several days. When it can be worked into smooth modeling consistency, it is ready for use and can be stored with the rest of the clay.

A special table, formica-top perhaps, may be used for clay activities, or clay boards of one-inch plywood (shellacked and waxed), or small breadboards which have had a coat of lacquer, or pieces of masonite may be used on other tables. As in all art activities, it is the part of good housekeeping to use newspapers to cover and protect equipment. The children can be more at ease in their work and can do a better job of cleaning up after their activities if plenty of newspapers are used.

Young children need to work with large chunks of clay. The only guidance necessary for them as they experiment with this medium is to explain that wetting the ends of the pieces of clay which they want to put together will help to hold them in place. Small jar lids with a little water in them may be placed on the table so that the children may share them as they work and have need of the water.

Play Doh

A commercial modeling compound known as Play Doh is clean, nontoxic, and quite pliable. It comes in white and the primary colors, which mix readily. It will harden completely in open air. Rolling pins and cookie cutters add to the pleasure of using this medium in the playhouse center. Play Doh must be stored in an airtight container to prevent it from drying out and hardening.

Polyethylene refrigerator dishes with tight-fitting lids make good storage containers. When the Play Doh becomes a little stiff it can be returned to its original soft and pliable consistency by dipping one's hands in water and then working the Doh with wet hands until all the moisture is absorbed.

Play Dough

Dough is an inexpensive and satisfactory modeling material. There are two kinds: salt and flour uncooked dough, and cooked dough. Both kinds may be stored in plastic bags in the refrigerator and used for days.

Besides modeling with the dough, children enjoy rolling it out on a breadboard and using different-shaped cookie cutters to create "beautiful" cookies which they bake in their play stove and serve to the dolls at teatime.

Recipes

Uncooked dough. Mix thoroughly one cup of flour and one cup of salt. Slowly add food coloring and enough water to this mixture until it becomes pliable. One tablespoon of salad oil added will keep the mixture from hardening. (If Christmas tree ornaments are to be made of this dough the salad oil should be omitted.)

Cooked dough. Mix one cup flour and ½ cup cornstarch into one cup cold water in a large bowl. Boil one cup salt and four cups water in a large pan. When boiling, pour salt water slowly into mixture in the bowl. Then return this milky-looking fluid to the pan and cook on low heat until thickened, stirring constantly (3-5 minutes). When cool, stir in 4-5 cups of flour. (If tempera paint is to be added for color, it should be added as the flour is added. If food coloring is to be used, it should be added before the flour is added. The colors should be bright and strong.) Then knead in more flour until the dough is soft and pliable, but not sticky.

If this dough draws moisture due to weather changes while stored, more flour may be kneaded into it. If it becomes too thick, more water may be worked into it.

Crayon Drawing

Large kindergarten crayons and large pieces of newsprint give children another means of telling what they are thinking and how they feel about it. (Remember, small crayons cramp young children's hands.) Soft wax crayons of a good quality give the best satisfaction. Because of the influence of coloring books in their homes since their "scribbling days," children at first may be lost without a picture to color. But with proper motivation they will soon find much greater satisfaction in "saying their story their own way" or in just making a pretty picture with their crayons and paper.

Drawing with Colored Chalk

Colored chalk, available in large sticks one inch in diameter, is a much freer medium than crayons. Experimenting with chalk can be a satisfying experience of control over the material and of producing vivid color effects. Children should always wash their hands thoroughly after using colored chalk.

While chalk may be used on wet or dry paper, teachers find that young children use the medium with more ease if they draw on wet paper. When buttermilk is used to moisten the paper, there is no need to use a fixative to prevent the chalk from smearing and rubbing off. The child may apply the buttermilk to his paper with a large easel brush. Manila drawing paper has a texture which makes interesting pictures, and it is more durable in quality than newsprint.

Printing

When given the materials and freedom to express their ingenuity, young children are able to do some very interesting designing in "printing." Very effective stamp pads can be made by using discarded aluminum frozen-food pans in which are placed scraps of felt which have been soaked in tempera paint. Either cloth (pieces of sheet) or paper may be used for the design. The printing may be done with any available shapes: small discarded blocks, jar rings, bottle caps, beads, large wooden spools, cardboard cylinders, a coarse vegetable brush, polyethylene squeeze bottles of different shapes, pieces of sponge, pieces of carrots, cut potatoes, clothespins, tongue depressors, ad infinitum.

Collages

Given a piece of cardboard, paste, and scrap materials of all kinds (cloth, wire, lace, small artificial flowers, string, yarn), the young child can make the most interesting "bumpy pictures." These are called collages. This activity stimulates the child's imagination and sets his creative powers to work.

Scissors

These need to be of good quality, sharp enough to cut paper easily. The scissors which are acceptable to children for use whenever they need them should be blunt-pointed. Activities calling for the use of scissors may include cutting out pictures from magazines, cutting out figures which the children have drawn or painted, and cutting paper or scraps of cloth for making interesting things which they like to create.

Free cutting for the sheer joy of manipulation will have priority over other cutting activities for the young child.

Paste

Some teachers prefer to keep library paste on hand, but in general they find that the most practical paste is that which they make up using wallpaper flour and cold water. This paste powder is available in small quantities (one-pound and five-pound bags) at most hardware stores and paint shops. It is practical for schoolroom use because it is inexpensive, quickly made, and easily cleaned up. One caution—because it sours, it is wise to make up one day's supply only. However, if there is paste left over it may be stored in the refrigerator for a few days.

When children are working with paste, they seem to feel the need to wash their hands frequently. Dampened paper towels placed where the children are at work are excellent for wiping little "pastey" fingers or removing excessive paste from their "pictures." Paste brushes are an asset for children in pasting activities.

Discarded Scrap Materials

Small cartons may be used for collecting and storing cardboard boxes of all sizes and shapes, scraps of cloth, buttons, lace, yarn, ribbon, feathers, spools, milk bottle tops, milk and ice cream cartons, and thread cones. A wallpaper sample book or two should be included among the discarded materials found useful in the school.

Construction Work

Equipment needed for woodworking activities are a worktable or bench, 3 hammers, 2 saws, 1 screwdriver, 1 plane, 2 brace and bits, 2 miter boxes, sandpaper of varying degrees of coarseness, nails

($\frac{3}{4}$", 1", $1\frac{1}{2}$"), plywood tool board with painted outlines of tools and with hooks for hanging in place, box of scrap wood of varying sizes of soft wood and free from splinters, wooden wheels, dowel sticks. Tools should be of good quality—not cheap toys, but of a size and weight which young children can handle easily.

If the woodworking activities can be carried on in an alcove of the room away from other activities, there is less danger of accident, and the necessary noise is not disturbing. This is also a good out-door activity, but *wherever it is carried on there should be close supervision by an adult.*

Block Construction

Unit blocks are conducive to a variety of self-expressional activities. Hollow blocks stimulate large muscular activities and dramatic play as the children create boats, jet planes, trains, buses, grocery stores, or farms. Low, open shelves for storage of blocks place the responsibility on the children for the housekeeping activities with this equipment.

In all the activities mentioned, emphasis has been on the creativity of the child's response to the materials. We should remember that to create, children must have experiences whether real or vicarious. Natalie Cole, in the opening sentence of her book *Arts in the Classroom,* reminds us that "children cannot create out of a vacuum."[7] Experiences are necessary to stimulate ideas.

A story, a trip to the zoo, a walk in the park, or perhaps a birthday party provides opportunity for a variety of responses. Each child brings into his present experience interpretations of past experiences in the group. Therefore, each child's response will be different if there is an atmosphere of freedom for creative self-expression.

"Guidance of little children during their art activities is concerned with both the establishment of good working habits and skills and with the maximum development of the child through his experiences in art. . . .

"The habits of work considered most desirable for kindergarten children to establish during their art activities appear to be the following: to procure and to store their own supplies; to work agreeably with other children in order to derive the fullest benefit from the use of art materials; and to respect the rights and property of others."[8]

Guidance of Art Experiences of Young Children

1. How can teachers and parents discover the meaning of children's art work when, in so many instances, "it" could be almost anything?

One never asks a young child *what* he has painted or *what* he is making. This not only does injury to his self-esteem, but it stifles the possibility of the child's sharing his interpretation of his creation. A more appropriate inquiry on the part of the adult might be: "What an interesting picture, Jane. Tell me about it."

2. When should the teacher show the child how to improve the expression of his thoughts with paint or clay?

One never "does over" the child's art work. Nor does one take a brush from the child's hand to "show him how." To do this would be interfering with the child's ability to think for himself and make his own discoveries. It would do harm to his initiative and his self-confidence both of which are essential for his optimum growth and development.

The teacher is concerned not so much with the child's art production as she is with what happens to the child as he creates with various materials.

3. Why are children's paintings and drawings so often all out of proportion?

The child will exaggerate in his paintings and drawings the thing of greatest importance to him. He draws in proportion to his feelings and not according to the reality of measurements. Tommy, drawing a picture of his new puppy, represented him twice as large as he represented the car which the puppy was chasing. "Out of proportion," we might say, so far as adult concepts are concerned, but "in proportion" to the emotion Tommy felt for his new puppy.

4. When the child works with clay, should he be encouraged to pull his figures out of his lump of clay instead of making parts and then sticking them together?

Viktor Lowenfeld in his book *Your Child and His Art* gives this answer: "It may never have occurred to you to watch how your child models in clay. . . . When Johnny makes a 'man,' he always makes the single parts first, the head, the body, two coils for arms, two for legs, and then he 'assembles' them by putting the single parts together. . . . This is the common way that children model. . . . It is very important that you do not influence your child to change his 'technique.' Thinking in 'single parts' is different from thinking of the 'whole,' and a superficially enforced change of 'technique' may confuse the child's thinking."[9]

5. Why don't we use patterns and hectographed outline pictures for children to color?

We do not believe in regimenting children's art work. We do not want children to be and think and perform just alike. We want to provide an atmosphere in the group which allows for individual differences in each child's personal expressions. If we condition children to patterns and hectographed materials, we do harm to their spontaneity and imagination and injure their ability in the realm of creativity.

Freedom to express his own ideas and feelings in his own way with paper, paints, clay, or other materials gives the child opportunity for emotional release. As he makes use of the art materials, he can project into his creation his feelings of anger, fear, or delight, and in so doing can gain some measure of relief.

Then when he has experienced accomplishment in making something all by himself, he gains a feeling of adequacy. The fulfillment of this important need of the individual child is essential for his emotional stability and social maturity. And therefore for him, school is so much fun!

Bibliography

Association for Childhood Education International, *Art for Children's Growing.* 3615 Wisconsin Ave., N. W., Washington 16, D. C., 1955.

Association for Childhood Education International, *Creating with Materials for Work and Play,* 1957.

Bannon, Laura, *Mind Your Child's Art.* New York: Pellegrini and Cudahy, 1952.

Gaitskell, Charles and Margaret, *Art Education in the Kindergarten.* Peoria, Ill. Chas. A. Bennett Co., Inc., 1952.

Jefferson, Blanch, *Teaching Art to Children.* Boston: Allyn and Bacon, Inc., 1959.

Lowenfeld, Viktor, *Your Child and His Art.* New York: The Macmillan Company, 1954.

Wills, Clarice D. and Stegeman, William H., *Living in the Kindergarten.* Chapter X, "Hands Can Tell Stories, Too." Chicago: Follett Publishing Company, 1956.

Experiencing Literature with Young Children

Through experiences with good literature for children, the young child sees life about him in word pictures which bring new and satisfying interpretations to him. His aesthetic sense is quickened, his intellectual growth is stimulated, and his knowledge is extended beyond his present environment as he enjoys happy times with a variety of stories and poetry. The child often begins to acquire a better understanding of himself as he identifies with the experiences of storybook children and adults. It is frequently quite a revelation to him to discover that other children have problems and joys, surprises and disappointments, not unlike his own.

The teacher of young children, sensitive to her group's needs and consuming interests, will have in readiness a variety of stories to use at the appropriate time. Some stories she will want to tell. Telling a story is often more effective than reading it, for the story-teller communicates the story with her eyes and facial expressions as well as with her voice. She can hold the interest and attention of the group more easily in telling a story, for, as she glances from child to child, she makes each one feel that she is speaking directly to him. There are books, however, which are meant to be read to children. Large, attractive picture books, when held so that all the group can see, have their distinctive place in the child's experiences with literature.

The child who has been introduced to good picture books in a group will find added pleasure in those same books as he "reads" them aloud to himself or to anyone who will listen and look with him. Large picture books without a text serve to stimulate the young child's imagination and encourage him to create his own stories.

Someone has very aptly said that the mind of the teacher of young children should be lined with poetry. Good anthologies of poetry for young children have among their word treasures just the right poem to fit almost any occasion. The teacher's familiarity with one or two good collections of poetry for children will mean that she can share with an individual or the group a bit of appropriate poetry which may highlight an experience or add a touch of humor to an incident. The teacher's love for and appreciation of poetry will surely "rub off" on the children.

In a happy, relaxed atmosphere creative poetry is always close by. Poetry, like music, flows in and out of the young child's work and play, emerging from some rich sensory experience to add beauty and sparkle to his activity.

Experiencing literature with the young child can introduce him to a whole new realm of good humor, beauty, and imagination, and can bring immeasurable pleasure and strengthen the bonds of friend-ship in the teacher-pupil relationships in a way unsurpassed by any other activity.

Selecting Books for Young Children

Children's book collections for a weekday church nursery or kindergarten should represent a wide variety of subject matter and types:

Some books will stimulate interest and enrich the child's vicarious experiences and background of knowledge.

Some books will help in the development of attitudes and concepts.

Some books will stimulate the child's imagination and creative responses.

Some will be for inspiration and spiritual enrichment.

Others will be sheer nonsense stories, just for fun.

A good collection of books for young children will be made up of books of varying sizes and shapes, having the following characteristics:

Books for young children should be well bound. They should lie flat when opened.

They should be made of good, tough-quality paper (not glossy in finish).

The illustrations should be simple, attractive in color and form, and should represent things familiar to the young child.

Books should be light in weight so that the young child can handle them with ease and satisfaction.

They should have appeal for adults as well as for children.

Sources of Book Lists and Book Reviews

Aids to Choosing Books for Your Children. Children's Book Council, 50 W. 53rd Street, New York 19, N. Y. (1 copy free)

Books of the Year for Children. An annual list. Child Study Association of America, Inc., 132 East 74th Street, New York 21, N. Y.

Children's Books for $1.25 or Less (revised annually) and *Bibliography of Books for Children* (revised annually). Association for Childhood Education International, 3615 Wisconsin Ave., N. W., Washington 16, D. C.

The Horn Book Magazine of Books and Reading for Children and Young People. Published at 585 Boylston St., Boston. Available for reference in public libraries.

Arbuthnot, May Hill, *Children and Books.* Chicago: Scott, Foresman & Company, 1957.

Before making out a purchasing list of books, the director should review each book to be certain it meets the qualifications of a good book and will meet the needs of the children. Consultation service may be enlisted from local librarians.

Social Science:

Beskow, Elsa, *Pelle's New Suit.* Ill. by author. New York: Harper & Brothers, 1929. A delightful picture book from Sweden for kindergarten children. Pelle wanted and needed a new suit. He had a pet lamb from which he cut the wool for his new suit. He has many experiences as the suit develops through the processes of the wool's being carded, spun, woven, dyed, and finally made into a lovely blue suit.

Brown, Margaret Wise, *The Little Farmer*. Ill. by Esphyr Slobodkina. William R. Scott, Inc., 1948, 1952. This little book helps a small child to know what it is like to live on a farm. He can see the little farmer on his own little farm, with cows, horses, and a barn, all on a small scale. Life on this small farm has the same problems and rewards that life on the big farm has. The child can get some concept of the interdependence of nature and man, people at work, and what security means.

Eng, Rita, *When You Were a Baby*. Ill. by Corinne Malvern. New York: Simon and Schuster, Inc., 1949. This book is written for the young child who may have a new baby at home. It will help the child to realize that once "a long time ago" he was a little baby and had to have lots of Mother and Daddy's attention.

Flack, Marjorie, *Story About Ping*. Ill. by Kurt Wiese. New York: The Viking Press, Inc., 1933. A delightful story, beautifully illustrated, about a little duck who lived on a Chinese houseboat. Ping has some interesting adventures. He was always the last one to get aboard the boat in the evening, and finally one time he was too late and the little boat went off without him.

Lenski, Lois, *The Little Airplane*. Ill. by author. New York: Oxford University Press, 1938. A simple little story of Pilot Small and his little airplane.

Puner, Helen Walker, *Daddies—What They Do All Day*. Pictures by Roger Duvoisin. New York: Lothrop, Lee & Shepard Co., Inc., 1946. This beautifully illustrated book shows a wide variety of jobs at which daddies work. It not only helps the child to understand about daddies and their work, but it gives some insight into the work in the community.

Shane, Harold and Ruth, *The New Baby*. Ill. by Eloise Wilkin. New York: Simon and Schuster, Inc., 1948. Mike and his family prepare for a new baby. He enjoys seeing big packages come to the house, bringing things for baby. Finally, a very large package comes. It is a big new bed for Mike. Mike gave his little bed to the baby.

Storybooks:

Association for Childhood Education International, *Told Under the Blue Umbrella*. Ill. by Grace Gilkison. New York: The Macmillan Company, 1933. This anthology of children's stories contains 26 familiar stories of acceptable versions for young children.

Mitchell, Lucy Sprague, *Here and Now Story Book*. New York: E. P. Dutton & Co., Inc., 1921. A book of stories for young children about their true-to-life experiences.

Mitchell, Lucy Sprague, *Another Here and Now Story Book*. New York: E. P. Dutton & Co., Inc., 1937. Similar to the book above.

Child Study Association of America, *Read to Me Storybook*. New York: Thomas Y. Crowell Company, 1947.

Child Study Association of America, *Read Me Another Story*. New York: Thomas Y. Crowell Company, 1949.

Child Study Association of America, *Read Me More Stories*. New York: Thomas Y. Crowell Company, 1951.

Excellent stories for reading to young children.

Science:

See section on "Experiencing Science with Young Children" for suggested books.

Religion:

See section on "Guiding the Religious Development of the Young Child" for books in this area.

Picture Books:

Berman, Rhoda, *When You Were a Little Baby*. Ill. by Mariana. New York: Lothrop, Lee & Shepard Co., Inc., 1954. Retraces in simple language and attractive pictures the growing-up of a baby. The story is told to a young child. It would be most effective in helping a child with a new baby at home to better understand that he, too, was once a little baby and had all the many things done for him that are being done for the new baby.

Bragg, Mabel C., *The Little Engine That Could*. Ill. by Lois Lenski. New York: The Platt & Munk Co., Inc., 1930. The colorful illustrations add charm to this delightful old story of the little engine who thought it could and it did.

Brown, Margaret Wise, *The Country Noisy Book*. Ill. by Leonard Weisgard. New York: William R. Scott, Inc., 1940. One of the Noisy Book series designed to help children to be aware of sounds, to listen to and identify them. (Record available.)

Brown, Margaret Wise, *Noisy Book*. Ill. by Leonard Weisgard. New York: William R. Scott, Inc., 1946. A simple little book, well illustrated, to help children learn to listen alertly to the sounds about them. (Record available.)

Brown, Margaret Wise, *ShhhBang, A Whispering Book*. Ill. by Robert de Veyrac. New York: Harper & Brothers, 1943. A hungry little boy wakes up a whispering little town with a big bang!

Bryant, Bernice, *Let's Be Friends*. Chicago: Childrens Press, Inc., 1954. A revised edition of *Everybody Likes Butch*. It is an excellent book to help young children through the emotional experience of starting to school and learning to be one of the group.

Burton, Virginia Lee, *Choo Choo*. Ill. by author. Boston: Houghton Mifflin Co., 1949. *Choo Choo* is a delightful picture book that tells the story of a runaway locomotive.

Evers, Alf and Helen, *Pokey Bear*. Ill. by the authors. Chicago: Rand McNally & Co., 1949. In this little book we learn that Father, Mother, and even Grandpa Bear were all slow, but little Pokey Bear was the slowest of all. Even a turtle won a race from him. One day a hawk swooped down at him. It scared him and he ran. It was so much fun running that he became the fast bear. Note: This book and *Crosspatch* have been published in one volume as two books. The publisher is E. M. Hale and Co., Eau Claire, Wisconsin.

Evers, Alf and Helen, *Crybaby Calf*. Ill. by the authors. Chicago: Rand McNally & Co., 1941, 1957. This well-illustrated story, with full-page drawings, is about a little calf who lived on the farm. Everybody on the farm was cheerful except the calf. He cried over everything, when it rained, when it was hot, when it was cold. One day he cried so much he sat in a pool of tears. It grew cold and his tears froze. While the farmer was trying to get the little calf loose he looked so funny the little calf began to laugh. He never cried again. Note: This book has been published in the same binding with *Fussbunny* by the same authors. The publisher is E. M. Hale and Co., Eau Claire, Wisconsin. The binding is superior to the single book publication by Rand McNally.

Fish, Helen Dean, *The Little Red Hen*. Ill. by Katherine Bernard. Boston: Houghton Mifflin Co., 1945. This is an amusing picture storybook. The old familiar folk tale is done in rebus-type picture story.

Flack, Marjorie, *Angus and the Ducks*. Ill. by author. Garden City, New York: Doubleday, Doran and Co., Inc., 1930. Story of a curious little Scottie dog who got into trouble with the ducks and decided not to be curious any more.

Flack, Marjorie, *Wait for William*. Ill. by Marjorie Flack and Richard A. Holberg. Boston: Houghton Mifflin Co., 1935. Four-year-old William couldn't keep up with the older children as they hurried to town to see the circus parade. His shoe came untied, so he had to stop and tie it. William was left alone, but when the circus came by, the man with the elephant gave William a ride. What fun to ride in the parade in front of the other children!

Flack, Marjorie, *Tim Tadpole and the Great Bull Frog.* Ill. by author. Garden City, New York: Doubleday & Company, Inc., 1948, 1959. Story of how Tim Tadpole grows in the pond and finally becomes a bull frog that can jump!

Flack, Marjorie, *Ask Mr. Bear.* Ill. by author. New York: The Macmillan Company, 1932. A little boy asks all the animals to tell him what to give his mother for a birthday present. The surprise ending of the gift Mr. Bear suggested delights young children.

Gag, Wanda, *Millions of Cats.* New York: Coward-McCann, Inc., 1928. An old man and an old woman wish for a cat. The old man went out in search of a cat. He came to a hill covered with cats. He couldn't decide which one to take and he didn't want to leave any so he took millions of cats. They drank up all the water in the pond and ate all the grass on the hill. When he reached home the old man and the old woman decided they couldn't feed that many cats. They said they would keep the most beautiful one. The cats all fought over who was the most beautiful until they ate each other up. Only one small kitten was left, so the little old woman and man finally had a kitten of their own.

Jones, Elizabeth Orton, *Little Red Riding Hood.* Ill. by author. New York: Simon and Schuster, Inc. This book is well written and beautifully illustrated for very young children. A good version for young children.

Kay, Helen, *One Mitten Lewis.* Ill. by Kurt Werth. New York: Lothrop, Lee & Shepard, Co., Inc., 1955. Lewis was always losing mittens—not both of them, only one. When he went out to play, Lewis wore mittens of different colors. The children called him "One Mitten Lewis." A new little girl had unmatched mittens, too, so she and Lewis put their mittens together to make pairs.

McCloskey, Robert, *Make Way for Ducklings.* Ill. by author. New York: The Viking Press, Inc., 1941. The story of Mr. and Mrs. Mallard who raise a family of ducklings by a lake in a big city park. The duck family has many exciting trips about town and causes traffic difficulties in the city.

Potter, Beatrix, *Tale of Peter Rabbit.* Ill. by author. New York: Frederick Warne & Co., Inc., 1903. This is the well-known classic of a little rabbit who just couldn't stay home like Flopsy, Mopsy, and Cotton Tail. He has some very exciting experiences in which he almost loses his life. He does lose his new clothes and catches a terrible cold.

Slobodkin, Louis, *One Is Good But Two Are Better.* Ill. by the author. New York: Vanguard Press, 1956. This is an excellent book for helping the child to grow more social in his attitudes and behavior. It is a most attractive picture book, with the script in verse. "One can swing alone in the sun, But you need two, To have more fun." It takes two to play store, ball, and hide-and-seek. It is a beautiful introduction to experiences of sharing work and play.

Squires, Elizabeth B., *David's Silver Dollar.* Ill. by Margot Austin. New York: The Platt & Munk Co., Inc., 1954. A satisfying, realistic story of David who received a silver dollar for his fifth birthday to buy whatever he wanted most in all the world.

Tresselt, Alvin R., *White Snow, Bright Snow.* Ill. by Roger Duvoisin. New York: Lothrop, Lee & Shepard Co., Inc., 1947. This is a lovely picture book describing the magical beauty of snowfall. Awarded the Caldecott medal.

Zion, Gene, *Really Spring.* Ill. by Margaret Bloy Graham. New York: Harper & Brothers, 1956. It was time for spring to come, but it had not. Everyone was unhappy because their city looked so dark and gray. A little boy said, "Why wait for spring to come and change everything to grass and flowers? Let's change it ourselves right now!" Everyone liked the idea, so they got together and painted daffodils on the houses and daisies on office buildings. The painted grass and flowers made the city look warm and springlike. That night a big rain came and washed away all the painted flowers. But a wonderful thing happened. There appeared something more beautiful—real spring. This is a good book for helping young children understand not only about the seasons, but also about a big city.

Poetry:

Association for Childhood Education International, *Sung Under the Silver Umbrella*. Ill. by Dorothy Lathrop. New York: The Macmillan Company, 1935. A delightful anthology of about 200 poems for young children from the modern writers as well as those of days gone by.

Aldis, Dorothy, *All Together*. New York: Putnam, 1952. The best of Dorothy Aldis' poems from three of her previous publications.

Brewton, John E., editor, *Under the Tent of the Sky*. New York: The Macmillan Company, 1937.

Milne, A. A., *When We Were Very Young*. Ill. by E. H. Shepard. New York: E. P. Dutton & Co., Inc., 1924. A delightful book of bubbling nonsense verse.

The Real Mother Goose. Ill. by Blanche F. Wright. Chicago: Rand McNally & Co., 1941. Most popular edition of Mother Goose.

Stevenson, Robert Louis, *A Child's Garden of Verses*. New York: World Book Co., 1946.

Concepts:

Barr, Jene, *Big Wheels! Little Wheels!* Ill. by Chauncey Maltman. Chicago: Albert Whitman & Co., 1955. One of the "concept" books for helping children understand how wheels help in work and play whether big or small.

Berkley, Ethel S., *The Size of It*. Ill. by Kathleen Elgin. New York: William R. Scott, Inc., 1950. How small is small? How tall is tall? Starting with first impressions of size, from little to big, the book develops in familiar terms the concept of size relationships. This is one of the "concept" books for the young child.

Berkley, Ethel S., *Ups and Downs. A First Book About Space*. Ill. by Kathleen Elgin. New York: William R. Scott, Inc., 1953.

Friskey, Margaret, *Chicken-Little-Count-to-Ten*. Ill. by Katherine Evans. Chicago: Childrens Press, Inc., 1953. This is an excellent picture book for giving basic concepts of numbers 1-10. Beautifully illustrated.

Green, Mary McBurney, *Is It Hard? Is It Easy?* Ill. by Lucienne Block. New York: William R. Scott, Inc., 1948. Young children can learn to value differences in each other if given the opportunity. They come to realize that each one has things that are easier or harder for them as compared to the group.

Zion, Gene, *All Falling Down*. Ill. by Margaret B. Graham. New York: Harper & Brothers, 1951. This builds the concept of "down" in a very appealing way. The rain, leaves, snow, etc., are pictured beautifully.

Chapter VII

The Program for Young Children (Part II)

Play as Education

Someone has said that play is the young child's most important business. Through it children relive experiences, clarify their understandings, enrich their vocabularies, and satisfy their need for feeling important and enjoying success. Play also serves as a "safety valve" for the individual child, for through such experiences he has opportunities to give vent to pent-up feelings and thus find release from tensions. Play activities also provide rich opportunities for children to develop physically—developing primarily the large muscles of their bodies.

Further analysis of the values of play experiences for kindergarten children reveals significant contributions to their spiritual development. In their playing together, children come to understand better themselves and their peers. And with this growing understanding comes the ability to put themselves in each other's position. They begin to appreciate the happiness which the group experiences as they learn to share, take turns, and discover means of solving their problems in peaceful ways.

Play can take on any one of several different forms in the living that takes place in the weekday church school: dramatic play, outdoor physical activities, rhythms, and loosely organized games.

Dramatic Play

Perhaps the simplest form of play is what we call dramatic play, in which the child identifies himself with his environment. He *is* whatever he *plays* he is. One minute he can be engrossed in "driving" a jet plane, then, with no difficulty at all, he can become a bus driver or the breadman delivering fresh bread to the "family" temporarily living in the playhouse center.

This type of play is one way the child has of handling his problem of being "little." In his play he is a big person, an important person, and plays out episodes and relationships that seem significant to him. He re-enacts family dramas most frequently, often reliving experiences which have been disturbing to him.

Another type of dramatic play which young children enjoy is play-acting very familiar stories. With neither costumes nor "props," a short story can come to life almost like magic. (This does not mean that the children have "parts" to say, nor are they given directions concerning their responses as they become the characters of the story. "Playing a story" in no way implies a performance!) The best experiences in play-acting for the young child are those times when the children "relive" a story, during the free play time on their own and without an audience.

Young children derive a great deal of satisfaction from dramatic play of all kinds, for they are always in control of the situation. They are learning much from such activity, as it provides firsthand experiences in the democratic way of living and presents real life situations in the group.

Imaginative, creative play fills a large portion of the young child's play life, provided his environment offers him creative play "tools." By tools are meant such equipment as building blocks of assorted sizes and shapes; toy cars, airplanes, trucks, and boats; "dress-up" clothes; cartons and wooden boxes of all sizes; child-size playhouse furnishings; woodworking equipment; and wooden animals and people. Mechanical toys are not included among the play "tools" used in the nursery school or kindergarten. Such toys set up definite limits in which children can find uses for them in their play, and they impose standards of action which children find impossible to attain with nonperforming toys. But what is still worse, mechanical toys stifle participation on the part of the children and hinder the development of their imagination and creative powers.

Outdoor Physical Activities

Fresh air and sunshine, an adequate play space, suitable play equipment, and an exuberance of joy are all conducive to the health and happiness of young children.

Outdoor equipment need be neither expensive nor elaborate. One large piece of climbing apparatus is adequate. The "climb around," a modified type of jungle gym, permits the child to climb upward at a slant, and after reaching the top he may slide down a pole in the center. Sand or sawdust should cover the ground under and around such equipment. The best outdoor equipment for the all-round development of the children is that which can be used creatively by them. In other words, it is unstructured—can be moved about easily and used in a variety of ways. Such equipment includes sawhorses of various heights (two of each height preferably), walking and jumping boards of different lengths; ladders, hollow blocks; empty, smooth crates, large packing boxes and barrels; wagons, wheelbarrows, and tricycles; and large beanbags and playground balls.

A large sandbox which can be covered at night and sunned during the day offers quiet play for individuals or a small group. Sand tools are needed, such as wooden or rubber shovels, small plastic buckets, wooden spoons, sifters, old colander and pans, rubber cars, boats, and other small toys.

A space at the edge of the yard should be provided for digging activities. In the springtime, the digging may grow into gardening experiences.

The outdoor space needs to be organized so that there is adequate room for safe use of the wheel toys and plenty of space for large-muscle play in the sunshine. If swings are used (*and they are not at all necessary*), special care must be taken to place them away from the free play area, and a fence should be placed around them to protect children from being hit by them. (Swings and seesaws are hazardous equipment for groups of young children. The danger involved outweighs their values.)

In their play experiences, children need blocks of time long enough to satisfy their play interests, but not long enough to allow them to become overstimulated and fatigued.

Games

Games afford fun and relaxation for the young child, and utilize the auditory, visual, and tactual senses as well as develop memory and concentration. They also provide a variety of opportunities for growth and development in motor and language skills; in social habits of taking turns, fair play, and co-operation; and in building meaningful concepts.

Games involving considerable bodily activity may be classified into the following groups as suggested by Foster and Headley:

". . . imitative games, choosing games, dramatic games, purely social games, and games of motor skill. . . . Games of a quieter sort, though not so numerous as the more active games, fill a felt need in the play program for young children. Most of these games have to do with the quickening of sense perception and with mental ability. Games involving little or no bodily activity may be divided into the following classes: games of hearing, games of touch, games of seeing, and guessing games."[1]

The following are suggested games, rhymes, and action songs which have been selected as representative of the kindergarten child's ability level and interest. (Games with as much organization as these would not be appropriate for the younger child.)

IMITATIVE GAMES

Did You Ever See a Lassie?

> "Did you ever see a lassie (laddie), a lassie, a lassie,
> Did you ever see a lassie do this way and that?
> Do this way and that way, and this way and that way,
> Did you ever see a lassie do this way and that?"

The children take hands and form a circle with one child standing in the circle. All sing together the first two lines. As they sing the last two lines, the children drop hands and try to imitate the child in the center who is doing some action, such as hopping first on one foot and then on the other, swinging arms back and forth, clapping hands in front and then over head, etc. Another child is chosen to stand in the circle as the song begins again. Music may be found in most kindergarten books.

Looby Loo

> "I put my right hand in,
> I put my right hand out,
> I give my right hand a shake, shake, shake,
> And turn myself about."
> Chorus:
> "Here we dance looby loo,
> Here we dance looby light,
> Here we dance looby loo,
> All on a day so bright."

Stanzas which follow with the chorus between each are:

> "I put my left hand in,
> I put my both hands in,
> I put my right foot in,
> I put my left foot in,

I put my both feet in,
I put my one head in,
I put my whole self in."

Holding hands, children skip around in the circle as they sing the chorus. As they begin each stanza, children drop their hands, face the center, and act out the words. Music for this game is given in *Singing Games* by Katherine Wessells, a Simon and Schuster "Little Golden Book."

PUNCHINELLO *

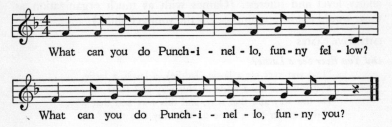

What can you do Punch-i - nel - lo, fun - ny fel - low?

What can you do Punch-i - nel - lo, fun - ny you?

"What can you do, Punchinello, funny fellow?
What can you do, Punchinello, funny you?"

Children form a circle with one chosen member in the center as Punchinello. As the children sing the first stanza Punchinello does something to be a "funny fellow" such as hopping on one foot, swinging his arms up and down, or anything that comes into his mind. The group then sings:

"We'll do it, too, Punchinello, funny fellow.
We'll do it, too, Punchinello, funny you."

This time the children in the circle imitate Punchinello. Then the group holds hands and walks around the circle while Punchinello chooses a child to take his place. The group sings:

"Whom do you choose, Punchinello, funny fellow?
Whom do you choose, Punchinello, funny you?"

Follow the Leader

One person is "It." Others fall in behind the leader and do everything he does. This game is very informal.

Simon Says

"It" stands before the group and performs one action after another. He says, "Simon says do this," after which the children must follow his action. When the leader just says, "Do this," the children do not move. This is a game which should be led by the teacher.

* Source unknown.

Exciting discoveries come from planting bulbs in the school garden.

"Stained-glass window" and open Bible provide a moment of worship.

Children arrange and rearrange manger scene as Christmas approaches.

A visitor from Ceylon extends horizons with stories of her land.

DRAMATIC SINGING GAMES

Here We Go 'Round the Mulberry Bush

Music in *Singing Games*, Katherine Wessells. A Simon and Schuster "Little Golden Book."

Fly, Little Blue Bird Through My Window

Children stand in a circle, joining hands and facing the center. One child is the Blue Bird. Children hold their hands as high as possible to form the windows. As the group sings the first stanza, the Blue Bird weaves in and out the circle, going under the arms (through the windows). On the second stanza children drop hands and clap in time to the song. The Blue Bird skips around and chooses another bird to follow him and the song starts over, this time with two birds flying in and out. The game continues until there are eight or ten birds "flying."

Five Little Chickadees

"Five little chickadees sitting in the door.
One flew away and then there were four.
Four little chickadees sitting in a tree.
One flew away and then there were three.
Three little chickadees looking at you.
One flew away and then there were two.
Two little chickadees sitting in the sun.
One flew away and then there was one.
One little chickadee left all alone.
He flew away and then there were none."

Five children sit in a row in front of the group. As each verse is sung, the chickadees in turn fly about over the room and then back to the larger group.

Music is found in *The Kindergarten Book*. Boston: Ginn and Company. For additional singing games refer to this book and to *Singing Games*. New York: Simon and Schuster Co.

SOCIAL GAMES

Shadow Tag

The children join hands and form a circle. One child is chosen to be the runner. He runs around the outside of the circle and touches another child who must run after the runner. If he can step on the runner's shadow, he catches the runner. (This is an outdoor game for a bright, sunny day.)

*Bushy Tail and Shiny Eyes**

A circle is formed. Two children are chosen as the squirrels, Bushy Tail and Shiny Eyes. They get down on all fours, facing each other in the center of the circle. They act out the poem which the children say together:

* Source unknown.

"Bushy Tail and Shiny Eyes sat in a hole in a tree.
Said Bushy Tail to Shiny Eyes, 'You can't catch me.' "
Hopping and running as squirrels, Shiny Eyes tries to catch Bushy Tail.

HEARING GAMES

Mother Cat and Baby Kitty

Two children lie in the floor in the center of the circle; one is the mother cat, and the other is the baby kitty. Someone tells the story: "Mother Cat and Baby Kitty had played and played. They were tired and lay down to rest. Mother Cat went sound asleep. Baby Kitty decided to slip away and hide. [Baby Kitty slips quietly outside of the circle and hides.] Then when Mother Cat woke up she missed Baby Kitty. She called, 'Meow!' [Baby Kitty must answer with a meow.]" When Baby Kitty is found, the game starts all over with a new mother cat and baby kitty.

Ring, Ring the Bell

One child in the group is chosen to hold a small bell. Another child is chosen to close his eyes. The child with the bell slips quietly to another part of the room. When the child is ready, the group calls out, "Ready." The child who has closed his eyes calls, "Ring, ring the bell." He listens as the other child rings the bell, then points in the direction from which he thinks the sound is coming. If he is not correct, he must choose someone to take his place. The bellringer has another time to play. If he is correct, he becomes the bellringer and another child is chosen to guess.

Sound Pattern Game

The teacher uses rhythm sticks or drum, or she may clap out sound patterns, and lets the children clap back the pattern. It is better for the teacher to give the pattern each time, for she will be more distinct and vary the patterns according to the ability of the children in the group. The following suggest a variety of patterns: (——·——) (·——·——·——) (··——) (···——) (··——··) [· means a short clap; —— means a long clap.]

Dog and Bone

One child is selected to sit on a chair with his back to the group. He is the dog. A small object is placed under his chair. The object represents a bone. He closes his eyes and listens for someone to come up and try to get his bone without being heard. If the dog hears a noise, he barks and points in the direction of the noise. If he is correct, he may choose another dog to take his place, and the game starts over. The entire group must learn that everyone must be very still to give the person who is trying to get the bone a fair chance to do so.

Huckle-Buckle Beanstalk

One child is chosen to step outside the room while another child hides a small object in the room and then slips quietly back to his place. The children begin clapping as a signal for the child who is outside to come into the room. As he searches for the object, the group claps. They clap softly when he is far away from the object and louder as he comes nearer to it. When he spies the object, he calls, "Huckle-Buckle Beanstalk," and goes to his place in the group. Two more children are then chosen, one to go out of the room and the other to hide the object. To vary the game and include more children, the teacher may select four or five to go out and hide. This would mean that the group then would not clap as the children searched.

VISUAL DISCRIMINATION GAMES

Finding Missing Parts

Each child has one of two parts of a picture. The pictures should be mounted on cardboard and cut in such a way that something is missing. For example, a picture of a barn might be lacking the roof, or a cat might be minus a tail. The children move about and try to find the child who has the other part of the picture. When the children are first introduced to this game, the teacher might start with only two or three pictures.

What Is Missing?

Four or five objects are placed on the floor in the center of the circle. One child is chosen to close his eyes while another child removes one object from the group. The child who was hiding his eyes tries to guess which object is missing. To make it a little more difficult, the objects may be moved around on the floor and then more than one object removed at a time.

Who Is Missing?

One child looks over the group and then hides his eyes. A child slips out of the room. The one chosen opens his eyes and tries to decide who left the room. The game may be made more difficult by letting two or three leave the room at a time.

GAMES OF TOUCH

Identifying Objects

Unknown to the children, the teacher has placed from 3 to 6 small objects (ball, toy car, toy airplane, pencil, key, penny, or other objects) in a cloth bag which is large enough to allow the objects to lie loosely in it. One at a time the children try to guess what the objects are by their sense of touch.

Identifying Children

One child is blindfolded. He stands in the center of the circle. Another child steps up and shakes hands with him. The blindfolded child attempts to identify the child by feeling his clothes and head.

GUESSING GAMES

Who Has the Shoe?

The group sits in a circle, close together with hands behind them. Children chant the words of the poem as the shoe is passed around the circle behind each child. One child in the center of the circle has his eyes closed until the end of the poem—"Tell me where my shoe is found." He has three guesses. If he guesses correctly, the child who has the shoe behind him becomes the cobbler and hides his eyes.

> Chant: "Cobbler, cobbler, mend my shoe.
> Have it done by half past two.
> Stitch it up and stitch it down.
> Tell me where my shoe is found."[2]

Button, Button, Who Has the Button?

One child goes around the circle slipping his hands, which he holds tightly together, through the tightly closed hands of each child in the circle. Somewhere in the group he drops the small object into a child's hands. The person guessing who has the "button" may hide it the next time. Seasonal variations may add interest to the game if small cardboard objects are substituted for the button, such as pumpkin, small red heart, little red bell, etc.

Sometimes I Am Tall, Sometimes I Am Small

One child stands with his back to the group. The group repeats and acts out the following words:

> "Sometimes I am very, very small.
> Sometimes I am very, very tall.
> Sometimes small, sometimes tall.
> Guess which I am now."

On the last line the group either stays down very small or stands on tiptoe very, very tall. If the child guesses correctly, he may choose another child to take his place and the game is repeated again.

Although games make a very definite contribution to the child's development, they should not be relied upon as a regular part of each day's procedure. They should be used informally as needs arise and the interest and ability of the group warrant such activity.

FINGER PLAYS

Finger plays should not take the place of children's poetry, for they are just interesting rhyming jingles accompanied by finger or hand movements. They have their place in the group activities of a nursery or kindergarten group. They help young children in the understanding of words and in vocabulary development. Finger plays encourage alertness and attentiveness and develop muscular control of the fingers. They are fun for the children and help them relax. They are helpful to use as a type of quiet transition for the group in changing from one activity to another.

The following are good sources of finger plays:

Institute of Child Welfare, University of Minnesota, *Finger Plays for Young Children.* Leaflet No. 11. Minneapolis, Minnesota.
Pierce, June, *The Wonder Book of Finger Plays and Action Rhymes.* New York: Wonder Books, Inc., 1955.
Jacobs, Frances E., *Finger Plays and Action Rhymes.* New York: Lothrop, Lee & Shepard Co., Inc., 1941.

Bibliography on Play

Hartley, Ruth E., *et al., Understanding Children's Play.* New York: Columbia University Press, 1954.
Hartley, Ruth and Goldenson, Robert M., *The Complete Book of Children's Play.* New York: Thomas Y. Crowell Company, 1957.
Kepler, Hazel, *The Child and His Play.* New York: Funk & Wagnalls Co., 1952.

Experiencing Science with Young Children

Plans for children in the weekday church group will include a wealth of experiences in science. The purposes of such experiences may be stated briefly:

to provide experiences which help the child to observe with all his senses and to sense the wonder and enjoy the beauty of God's world;

to give him opportunities for growing in the scientific method of thinking and to find answers to his questions through experimentation and the use of such sources as people and pictures; and

to help the child trace the beauty and the wonders of the world about him to God, the Giver of all life.

In attempting to realize these purposes in the group's day-by-day living, the teacher will provide an environment which is rich in varied experiences that stimulate curiosity and inquiry on the part of the child. Such an environment must also allow him freedom for investigating, exploring, and experimenting.

Science Center

A table or shelf, easily accessible to the children, may be known to them as the "science center." The children should be encouraged to bring to school interesting "discoveries" to share with the group.

Something new should be found each week in the science center—seeds, sea shells, rocks, old bird's nests, germinating seeds, flowers, caterpillars, frog eggs or tadpoles, etc.—whatever is seasonal and within the child's ability to understand and appreciate.

Children can discover answers to many of their questions through simple experimentation. For example, they often fret over a rainy day which makes necessary a change in their plans for the day. To help them answer their question, "Why does it have to rain anyway?", the teacher might interest the group in discovering for themselves a need for rain. They might plant some corn in two flowerpots, leaving one pot dry without ever watering it, and watering the other one every few days. The results of such an experiment soon show the children that with the rain God is providing plant and animal life a needed drink of water which is essential to the production of food and maintenance of life. Instead of being disappointed and cross because the rain spoiled some outdoor plans, young children can see the part it plays in the life of the world, can experience real gratitude for it, and at the same time can learn tolerance. So many learnings take place in one experience!

Gardening Activities

Indoor gardens may be planted in any number of ways. A simple glass jar garden is fascinating for the children to make and observe. All that is needed is a wide-mouth gallon jar and some ferns, moss, and other small plants. Turn the jar on its side, spread about two cups of moist sand in the jar, and arrange the mosses and plants on the sand. When the children have completed the garden arrangement, they need to sprinkle it lightly with water, then screw the lid on tightly. If the jar is placed in the sunshine for part of the day, it will not need watering. If mold appears in the garden, it is an indication that there is too much moisture in the jar. Leaving the lid off for a few hours will allow for the needed evaporation.

Other indoor gardening activities might include planting large lima beans in paper drinking cups; starting avacado seeds in shallow dishes of water; and placing a sweet potato in a jar of water, leaving about half of the potato sticking up out of the water. Dish gardens of carrot tops are always interesting. (Cut off the top of the carrot, leaving about two inches of the stem and one inch of the carrot. Stand several of these up in a shallow dish of water and watch the fernlike shoots of green which will continue to grow for several weeks.) Growing plants from cuttings is another activity which helps children learn through experience ways in which plant life is continued. It is enlightening for the children to watch large lima beans sprout on moist cotton placed in a shallow pan.

Flower seeds may be planted in large flowerpots and cared for indoors until it is time to transplant them in the outdoor garden. During an experience of planting seeds and raising plants the child begins to understand how plant life is reproduced. He can also be helped to know that God expects us to help Him carry out His plans for growing things.

Every group needs an outdoor garden—a small plot of ground, very near the outdoor play area, where the children can dig, plant seeds and bulbs, and care for growing flowers and vegetables. In selecting seeds and bulbs for planting, it is well to be certain that the plants will have time to mature before the school term is over. Having flowers to enjoy and to share and a harvest of vegetables to gather is a very important part of the gardening experience (even if the "harvest" is just radishes, lettuce, and onions). The children can feel a real sense of joy as they watch their garden grow and are led to appreciate the wonder of God's provision for our needs. Such an experience will also help the children realize that they are workers with God in His world.

Nature Activities

Another *must* for the kindergarten is a "balanced" aquarium (stocked with fish, growing water plants to replenish the necessary supply of oxygen for the fish and to use up the excess of carbon dioxide, and snails or other scavengers to keep the aquarium clean). If the fish bowl or aquarium is balanced and is kept out of direct sunlight, it will not need to be cleaned or to have the water changed more than once every few months. When water is added to the aquarium, it should first be allowed to stand in a bowl for a day.

A terrarium will provide opportunity for experiences such as observing and caring for a land turtle, snails, small plants, insects, and cocoons. A simple terrarium may be made by using a large oblong aquarium and making a wire screen cover for it.

Animals are important "inhabitants" and visitors in the school. A rabbit is an interesting pet to care for, particularly in the springtime when he can live in an outdoor hutch or pen. He needs a bowl for water and one for food. He will eat dry oatmeal, carrots, lettuce, and special rabbit food. Care needs to be taken that his pen makes him safe from dogs. Golden hamsters are easy to have in the kindergarten room and are always fun to observe.

CARING FOR GOLDEN HAMSTERS

A hamster must have a metal cage, since he can chew his way out of a wooden box. Special hamster cages equipped with drinking bottle and exercising wheel may be purchased at pet stores.

Care. Cover the floor of the cage with cedar chips. Shred several paper hankies for the hamster to use in making his bed. Keep the cage out of drafts and in room temperature of around 70°-72°.

Food and water. Keep his jar of water filled. He will suck the water out of the tube as he needs it. He should be fed daily. When fed, he will stuff his pouches on either side of his mouth full and then go to his "kitchen," a special place in his cage where he stores his food. He eats it when he needs it and only what he needs, so there is no danger of overfeeding him. He likes prepared hamster food (mixed grains), raw potatoes and apples, dry bread and dog biscuits.

The male makes the best pet as he has the better disposition. After the hamster is about a month old he may be handled gently a little every day until he becomes accustomed to being played with. He will bite if he is handled carelessly. Little children enjoy watching the hamster's antics in the cage just as much as playing with it.

Female hamsters are capable of bearing young at about seven weeks. The babies are very tiny little creatures. The cage should not be cleaned after they are born until they are taken away from their mother at about three weeks.

CARING FOR BOX TURTLES

During the spring months box turtles may be found in woods, fields, meadows, and on the open road. A box turtle makes an interesting pet for the group. He can be cared for indoors or out. A large wooden box makes an acceptable terrarium.

The turtle likes dried grass or leaves to hide in and a shallow container for drinking water. The box turtle is a land turtle so he does not want a swimming pool. He will enjoy having an outdoor pen for exercise. His food can consist of raw apples, bananas, hardboiled eggs, lettuce, ground beef, and food scraps. Children should not try to feed the turtle by hand, for it might bite their fingers.

CARING FOR TADPOLES

Frog eggs (a mass of eggs that look like gelatin) may be found along the edges of quiet streams or ponds in the spring of the year. They may be taken to the schoolroom so the children can observe the eggs as they hatch. Pond water and a little mud from the bottom of the stream are needed. Stones, small sticks, and leaves from the stream should be added to the tadpole aquarium since they contain tiny plants which the young tadpoles eat.

When the tadpoles hatch they may be fed a little prepared goldfish food and a little yolk of a hard-boiled egg every few days. Food which isn't eaten in a couple of hours should be removed.

When the tadpoles begin to absorb their tails and get their big jumping legs, they should have a rock or stick on which to climb when they feel the need to get out of the water temporarily.

Watching the physical changes of the tadpole is fascinating to the young child.

OBSERVING INSECTS

Bugs and butterflies may be observed for short times and then released to their native habitat. A simple container for bugs, caterpillars, and butterflies can be made by using two round metal cake pans for the top and bottom and putting between them a roll of screen wire about ten inches in width. The wire roll may be stapled together or fastened in place by "sewing" the wire with a piece of copper wire. Another simple cage for small insects and caterpillars is made by covering the top of a lamp chimney with screen wire by means of adhesive tape, and placing it over a small potted plant.

Preparing Simple Foods

Experiences in preparing several simple foods can have numerous science learnings for young children. Making a Jello dessert is an activity which holds interest for the children as they observe its change of consistency. Other cooking activities might include baking cookies and making fruit sauce. Discovering the source of butter by churning sour cream in an old-fashioned churn offers a delightful surprise for the children. If a glass churn is available, the children will be able to watch the "butter come" and see it gather around the dasher. And oh, how good it tastes when worked, salted, and spread on crackers!

Young children enjoy a variety of water-play activities. They gain considerable satisfaction in discovering what they can do with water and in sensing control over it. A piece of small rubber hose and two pails are all the equipment necessary for the children to experience a thrill over siphoning water. This scientific process can be used by the children in changing the water in the aquarium.

Providing a stimulating environment for kindergarten children will mean an extension beyond the classroom. Excursions may be taken to gather colored leaves and interesting seeds, to look for cocoons in the fall, to find the first spring flowers, or frog eggs or tadpoles in a shallow stream. The group may take a trip to the zoo, a flower shop, a farm, a pet shop, or a nearby park. There is so much to discover when one is four or five years old!

While excursions are important in adding to the child's fund of knowledge and experience, the teacher remembers too that the immediate environment holds almost unlimited possibilities for science experiences. For example, observing the kinds of weather; watching birds in the play yard and helping to care for their needs in each season—keeping water in the bird bath, putting out food for them, especially in winter, and in early spring scattering nest-building materials, bits of string and cloth, cotton and straw.

In all of the science activities, the teacher's attitude toward inquiry and exploring the unknown is of primary importance in stimulating the instinctive curiosity of the children. Adults need to remember that children are scientists. In the weekday church nursery school or kindergarten the teacher has many splendid opportunities for giving young "scientists" Christian interpretations of their everyday science experiences.

Many of the richest experiences in science will come unexpectedly during the session from some interest or need of the group. The opportunities for science activities in the following outline are in no way suggested as an outline of a year's work, but are merely indicative of the kinds of science interests that may develop in the weekday groups. The nursery teacher will select those activities which best meet the needs of her group of three-year-olds.

Seasonal Activities

A. *Autumn*
    1. Possible observations concerning:
       a. Weather

The days are becoming cooler.

Dark comes earlier in autumn.

Frost often forms on the grass and plants during the night.

b. Animals

Some birds fly away to warmer places for the winter.

In autumn some animals grow heavier coats of fur.

In autumn some animals store food for the winter.

In autumn there aren't as many insects as in summer.

c. Plants

In autumn leaves of many trees become brightly colored.

In the late autumn many trees lose their leaves.

In autumn seeds of many plants ripen.

Different kinds of seeds travel about in many different ways.

2. Group experiences:

a. Discussions of observations such as changes in the weather, seed distribution, frost on the ground.

b. Collecting and examining seeds, cocoons, colored leaves, empty bird's nests, etc.

c. Hearing stories and singing songs about autumn.

d. Sharing experiences about week-end trips to mountains or country with family; bringing plants into the house at night to avoid frost; and buying warmer clothes to wear.

e. Excursions to park to observe trees, birds, squirrels, etc. (Watch squirrels gathering nuts.)

f. Experimenting with seeds to find out what is inside. (Use large lima beans—soak and open to see baby plant.)

g. Preparing and serving some fall foods, such as popcorn, apple sauce, and apple jelly.

h. Looking at picture books with illustrations about children's experiences in autumn; looking at projected slides and filmstrips about autumn activities.

i. Watching caterpillars spin cocoons.

j. Getting cuttings of geranium, coleus, and begonia before frost and placing in glasses of water to watch sprout.

B. *Winter*

1. Possible observations concerning:

a. Weather

Winter follows autumn.

The days are cold.

The sun does not feel as warm in winter as it did in autumn and summer.

The days are shorter; night comes earlier.

Ice and snow become water when melted.

b. Animals

People help take care of some animals in winter.

Some animals live on the food they stored away during the autumn months.

Cocoons live quietly through the winter.

It is harder for birds to find food in winter.

Some animals grow extra warm coats for winter.

c. Plants

Some plants which lose their leaves have buds for next spring's leaves.

Some plants die but their roots live under the ground and send up new plants in the spring.

2. Group experiences:

a. Discussing the first hard freeze of the season; frost on the window panes; children watching their breath out of doors; children's new warm sweaters, mittens, boots, etc.

b. Making a simple feeding station for birds and keeping food in it.

c. Watching the differences in the thermometer indoors and out.

d. Keeping a weather chart, putting up pictures illustrating the kind of weather for each day.

e. Observing snow crystals through magnifying glasses.

f. Experimenting with water in freezing weather—freezing water in a jar with a lid on it; blowing soap bubbles outdoors and watching them freeze.

g. Hearing stories and singing songs about experiences of wintertime.

h. Making a terrarium in an empty aquarium or gallon jar with a tight lid. Small plants, mosses, and ferns will continue to grow without any care.

i. Planting various kinds of plants in water—bulbs, sweet potato, avocado seeds, tops of turnips and carrots, etc., and watching the growth. (Cut off the top half of carrot, beet, or turnip and place in shallow dish of water to observe the attractive foliage which grows.)

j. Enjoying pictures in books, 3-D pictures in View-Master, and projected pictures about life during wintertime.

k. Experiences connected with physical science, as: playing with magnets to observe the behavior of different kinds of objects when placed near the magnet; striking glasses filled with varying amounts of water to note differences in pitch; playing with different-size drums to observe tone and pitch; playing with prism and mirror to observe the behavior of sunlight; observing machines in construction; using pulley and wheels in construction work in kindergarten.

C. *Spring*

1. Possible observations concerning:
   a. Weather
      Spring follows winter.
      The days are growing warmer.
      The days are becoming longer.
      Dark doesn't come as soon in spring as it did in winter.
      The sun is warmer than it was in winter.
      There are many rainy days in spring.
      The wind blows very hard in early spring.
   b. Animals
      Birds build their nest homes.
      Birds lay eggs and hatch families of baby birds.
      Baby animals of many kinds appear in spring.
      Moths and butterflies emerge from their cocoons.
   c. Plants
      Plants that lived through winter begin to grow again.
      Seeds grow into new plants.
      People plant gardens in the spring.
      Buds on trees begin to burst; fruit trees bloom.
      Plants need sunshine, water, and air to grow.
2. Group experiences:
   a. Plant a small vegetable garden and care for it.
   b. Plant grass seeds in a sponge placed in shallow dish of water.
   c. Raise tadpoles.
   d. Plant large lima beans on wet cotton to observe them sprout.
   e. Set a hen and care for her, keeping a record of days it takes the eggs to hatch.
   f. Take a walk to look for signs of spring—flowers, new little leaves, etc.
   g. Observe cocoons hatch and moths lay eggs.
   h. Take an excursion to a pet shop, a greenhouse, or to a farm.
   i. Observe birds building nests and getting food for babies.
   j. Observe an ant colony which has been caught and placed in a narrow glass container and then placed in the dark for several days.
   k. Observe the thermometer, watching the mercury rise.
   l. Enjoy hearing stories and singing songs about experiences in spring.
   m. Experiment with wind, feeling it as it turns a pin wheel. (Make a kite and try flying it.)
   n. Enjoy audio-visual materials about experiences in springtime.
   o. Keep a weather chart on a large calendar, putting up pictures of the kind of weather each day.
   p. Observe how leaves on plants turn toward the sun.

Resource Materials

1. Large nature pictures in Kindergarten Picture Set, from Denominational Boards.
2. 2″ x 2″ slides of birds, moths, flowers, and animals. Society for Visual Education, 327 South La Salle Street, Chicago, Illinois.
3. Album: "American Bird Songs," Ithaca, New York: Comstock Publishing Co.
4. Color filmstrips—"Autumn Is Here"; "Winter Is Here"; "Spring Is Here"; "On the Farm"; "Out of Doors"; "At the Zoo"; "Farm Animals and Pets"; "Homes of Birds." (All from S. V. E., Chicago, Ill.)
   Stories About the Seasons, Kit No. 1, Family Filmstrips, Inc. "Playing in the Rain"; "Picnic in the Country"; "God's Autumn World"; "God's Care in Winter." (Available at Denominational Boards.)
5. View-Master and projector for View-Master reels. Reels about songbirds; flowers of fall, summer, and spring; butterflies and moths; animals of the zoo, farm animals; and wonders of the deep.
6. Equipment for science experiences in the kindergarten:

balanced aquarium (fish, water plants, sand, snails, other scavengers)
terrarium for plants and small animals (small turtle or horned toad)
animal cage
several kinds of magnets—bar, U, horseshoe
large thermometer
magnifying glasses
prism
mirror—round, shaving type
compass
electric hot plate
½″ rubber tubing
bicycle pump
field glasses
pulley and rope
yardstick
3″ funnel
4 pieces of plate glass 8″ x 10″— edges bound with masking tape
2 shallow 10″ x 12″ aluminum baking pans
flowerpots
wide-mouth gallon jar
medicine dropper
two 8″ round cake pans
watering can
sponges—cellulose
lamp chimney—large
gardening tools
hourglass
old clock with alarm
old scales
old locks and keys
corks
wire
jars
round ice cream cartons
paper cups
screen wire
small boxes
paper milk containers
calendar
masking tape
plaster of Paris
drinking straws
vegetable and flower seeds
glycerine
fruit for cooking—apples, prunes

Books for the Teacher

Comstock, Anna B., *Handbook of Nature Study*. Ithaca, N. Y.: Comstock Publishing Associates, 1947.

Science in Childhood Education. New York: Teacher's College, Columbia University, 1944.

Foster, Josephine and Headley, Neith, *Education in the Kindergarten*. New York: American Book Company, 1948, revised 1959. Chapter XVIII.

Gans, Roma, Stender, Celia, *et al.*, *Teaching Young Children in Nursery School, Kindergarten, and the Primary Grades*. Yonkers, New York: World Book Co., 1952. Chapter X.

Garrison, Charlotte G. and Sheehy, Emma D., *At Home with Children, The Guide to Pre-School Play and Training*. New York: Henry Holt & Co., Inc.

Haupt, Dorothy, *Science Experiences for Nursery School Children*. N. A. N. E. Distribution Center, Union of Rhode Island, Kingston, Rhode Island, 1957.

Heffernan, Helen, *Guiding the Young Child*. Boston: D. C. Heath & Company, 1951, 2nd edition 1959. Chapter VII.

Hochman, Vivienne and Greenwald, Mildred, *Science Experiences in Early Childhood Education*. New York: 69 Bank Street Publications. Bank Street College of Education, New York City.

Hyde, Margaret Oldroyd and Keene, Frances W., *Hobby Fun Book*. Pelham, New York: The Seahorse Press, Inc., 1952.

Sheehy, Emma D., *The Fives and Sixes Go to School*. New York: Henry Holt & Co., Inc., 1954. Chapter XI.

Zim, Herbert S., *This Is Science*. Washington, D. C.: Association for Childhood Education International, 1945.

Zim, Herbert S., *Science for Children and Teachers*. Washington, D. C.: Association for Childhood Education International, 1953.

Science Books for Young Children

Blough, Glenn O. and Parker, Bertha Morris, *Animals Around the Year*. Evanston, Ill.: Row, Peterson & Company, 1955.

Graig, Gerald S. and Burke, Agnes, *Science All About Us*. New York: Ginn & Company, 1950.

Graig, Gerald and Bryan, *Science and You*. Atlanta: Ginn & Company, 1955.

Huntington, Harriet E., *Let's Go Outdoors*. New York: Doubleday & Company, Inc., 1939.

Huntington, Harriet E., *Let's Go to the Seashore*. New York: Doubleday & Company, Inc., 1941.

Huntington, Harriet E., *Let's Go to the Brook*. New York: Doubleday & Company, Inc., 1952.

Lenski, Lois, *I Like Winter*. New York: Oxford University Press, 1948.

Lenski, Lois, *Now It's Fall*. New York: Oxford University Press, 1948.

Lenski, Lois, *Spring Is Here*. New York: Oxford University Press, 1948.

Parker, Bertha Morris and O'Connell, Mabel, *Fall Is Here*. Evanston, Ill.: Row, Peterson & Company, 1953.

Parker, Bertha Morris and O'Connell, Mabel, *Spring Is Here*. Evanston, Ill.: Row, Peterson & Company, 1953.

Parker, Bertha Morris and O'Connell, Mabel, *Summer Is Here*. Evanston, Ill.: Row, Peterson & Company, 1955.

Parker, Bertha Morris and O'Connell, Mabel, *Winter Is Here*. Evanston, Ill.: Row, Peterson & Company.

Pistorius, Anna, *What Bird Is It?* Chicago: Wilcox & Follett Co., 1947.

Pistorius, Anna, *What Animal Is It?* Chicago: Wilcox & Follett Co., 1947.

Selsam, Millicent, *All Kinds of Babies and How They Grow*. New York: William R. Scott, Inc., 1953.
Webber, Irma E., *Up Above and Down Below*. New York: William R. Scott, Inc., 1943.
Webber, Irma E., *Travelers All, The Story of How Plants Go Places*. New York: William R. Scott, Inc., 1944.

Language Development

Seated at the book table in a weekday church kindergarten, five-year-old Bobby was deeply engrossed in a lovely new copy of *Angus and the Ducks*. To an adult's questioning, "What are you reading?", Bobby quickly responded, "I can't read yet, but I can do a lot of thinking."

It is evident that Bobby was on the right road to reading, for educators today agree that it is "reading as an interest, not as a skill"[3] that should be deeply rooted in the child's kindergarten experience.

In years past there have existed two extreme views with regard to *reading and the kindergarten:* the first denied any consideration of the contribution of kindergarten experiences to the child's success in beginning first grade reading; the second was a definite attempt to incorporate formal reading instruction at the kindergarten level. *Experience has shown the fallacies of both concepts.*

Research studies indicate that results of formal reading readiness experiences in the kindergarten have proved that premature instruction was either "impermanent" or tended to "interfere later with success" in the learning of the skills. Too often the young child became so discouraged over his difficulty with the task of reading that he came to think of himself as a complete failure at the very onset of his educational experience. This was a threat to his self concept and sense of security, and detrimental to his attitude toward books, reading, and life in general.

Education today recognizes that readiness for reading is not something which can be "built in" the child through a so-called readiness program. A wise program for five-year-olds will have no time for reading readiness workbooks, readiness gadgets, or hectographed exercises and drills. Such materials as those which have the child color the little house red or put a mark on the tallest boy in the row or draw a circle around the ducks that are just alike are artificial activities which waste the school's money and the children's and teacher's time. In the day's program they displace the good learning experiences which five's could be enjoying. They crowd out those enriching experiences which the children should be having *now* because they are ready for them *now*.

Teachers and parents need to remember that the youngsters are always ready for something because they are growing. Giving them an environment in which to enjoy those experiences for which the children are now ready will mean that the children live richly each today. This is the best possible utilization of the child's time and energies in the important days before he is ready to read.

A good kindergarten program will offer the children many natural opportunities to enjoy a wealth of firsthand experiences. Paul Witty points out the following contribution which firsthand and vicarious experiences make to the child's first grade reading activities:

"Experiences help children understand the material they are going to read at school. The more understanding and information a child can *bring to a book*, the more he will *get out of it*. The more varied a youngster's experiences, the more meaning there will be in what he reads."[4]

The following are illustrative of some of the firsthand experiences which may be provided for the child in the weekday church kindergarten:

Excursions. The teacher would want, first of all, to help the child feel at home in his new environment. He will need to become acquainted with the rest of the building and the church workers whom he will be seeing from day to day. This may mean several short excursions through the church building, each with a different purpose. One day the group may go into the sanctuary to enjoy the stained-glass windows, or to listen as the organist plays some lovely music. Another excursion may be taken to acquaint the group with the church personnel, where they work and what they do. Knowing especially the custodian, where he may be found and what he does for the welfare of the kindergarten, is very important for the child's development of attitudes of respect and for his appreciation of helpers in the church.

Short excursions into the community may take the form of nature walks to enjoy the pretty colored leaves in the fall, to visit a neighbor's new family of puppies, or just to "see what they can see." Longer excursions will depend upon the children's background— their needs and interests and the resources available in the community. Among the places of greatest interest for the five-year-old are: the zoo, pet shop, fire station, florist, farm, and railroad station— with, perhaps, a short train ride. Care must always be taken to avoid fatigue and overstimulation in the children.

Excursions, besides enriching the child's concepts and fund of knowledge, give the group common experiences about which to think and talk. There will be planning times together when the teacher and the children discuss what they want to see and ways of acting on the excursion.

Follow-up activities will take many forms according to the interests aroused by the discoveries made during the excursion. There will, of course, be discussions and a thank-you letter which the children will dictate and send to the host who entertained them. Usually dramatic play will follow an interesting excursion, and sometimes this will work into a center of interest for the group. Most well-planned excursions lend themselves to follow-up experiences through a variety of expressional activities.

A large storybook may be made, using pictures the children draw or paint. The teacher will manuscript the "stories" which the children dictate about things that happened on their trip. Together the teacher and the children make a large, interesting storybook. These stories may be read back to the children as a story from any other book would be. *The children are not to be taught to read these stories!*

Resource People. Another means of helping the young child to become better acquainted with the community is to bring some of the community helpers into the school. One very practical approach to this is to work through the parents and the occupations they represent. The experience will be more meaningful all around when the community helper who visits in the kindergarten is a mother or father of one of the children in the group. Such helpers might include the minister, a musician, doctor, policeman, nurse, librarian, carpenter, grocer, fireman, or florist.

To ensure the best possible learning experience, the group would follow much the same planning and follow-up procedures as indicated for the activities built around the excursion.

Everyday Activities in the Kindergarten. New concepts are gained by participation in the everyday work and play activities, in such experiences as caring for pets and plants, and in the responsibility for helping to keep the room attractive and the work and play materials in order.

Social adjustment and language development grow out of experiences such as birthday celebrations, special parties (Halloween, Christmas, Valentine's Day), sharing experiences, entertaining younger children and the kindergarten parents, rhythm activities, and dramatic play.

Creative Activities. Freedom in experimenting with a variety of media offers the child opportunities to give expression to his thoughts and feelings. Sometimes he retells a story or an incident with his paintbrush, clay, crayons, or scrap materials. Through such activities he is learning to communicate ideas before he has an adequate vocabulary for verbalizing. Co-operative enterprises in construction, either with blocks or in woodworking activities, provide opportunities for growth in interpersonal relations and stimulate spontaneous conversation.

The kindergarten child may gain a vast store of information and understandings through vicarious experiences by such means as: stories, poems, movies, dramatization, flat pictures (projected and nonprojected), three-dimensional stereograph pictures, and discussion of activities.

The child's speaking vocabulary develops as a result of all his meaningful experiences. The emphasis here is on "meaningful experiences." Just "seeing" and "hearing" and "speaking" will not guarantee a growth in meaningful vocabulary. Understanding must accompany the experience. To illustrate, a group of kindergarten children were setting an old hen one spring day not long after Easter. There had been very little preparation for the activity and no discussion following. It was not strange, then, that Ronnie should have explained to his mother when she came for him: "Mother, guess what! We hid Easter eggs under a chicken today."

As the kindergarten teacher observes small group conversations, she needs to be alert to catch vocabulary needs and to plan wisely to help the child gain correct meanings. For example, a kindergarten child playing in the shade of a large tree on the play yard asked, "Where do oak trees come from?" To which an all-wise five-year-old shared his knowledge, explaining, "Why okra, ya dumb bunny! Anybody knows that." This incident, overheard by the teacher, stimulated some very interesting activities out of which came many new usable words for the entire group of children, as well as the corrected scientific fact for the two youngsters involved in the original conversation.

Through the daily experiences in the group the child has opportunity to grow in his ability to communicate his ideas in simple sentences. The teacher's job is to provide a permissive atmosphere in which the child enjoys freedom to talk as he works and plays. The following are suggestive of a few of the language activities in which the children engage normally and naturally in the daily program:

retelling stories and creating original ones
planning and evaluating group experiences
creating jingles and poems
playing stories and songs
talking over toy telephones to each other
sharing experiences with the group
talking with teachers and peers during work and play
dictating letters and invitations
dictating stories to be recorded by the teacher in the large group record book.

Lucille Harrison cites the values of the child's enlarging his vocabulary and his ability to communicate in complete sentences:

"The development of a broad vocabulary and the ability to use simple English sentences are the best-known weapons against the development of a word-calling, meaningless type of reading so often heard in the primary grades."[5]

Besides having experiences which help the child grow in his ability to communicate ideas, he needs opportunities for learning to listen actively and courteously to the expressed ideas of others in the group. Unless a child listens actively, he doesn't really hear. And unless he "hears," he is not able to follow directions or gain the understandings which the experience of active listening has to offer.

Of greatest importance in the classroom environment for stimulating the child's interest in books and reading is the teacher and her attitudes toward books and reading. As she manifests pleasure and appreciation for books and interest in reading, she is setting a worthy example for the child to emulate.

She will arrange, in a light, cheerful corner of the kindergarten room, a library for the children. Near the shelves on which the books are kept and displayed she may have a small table around which three or four children may sit and enjoy "reading" and discussing their picture books. She will exercise judgment in the number and kinds of books she has available for the children at one time. Each week she will put out two or three volumes which are new to the children and will put away for a few weeks books of which the children may have become tired.

As the child hears fascinating stories read from books and as he himself looks at books, he comes to realize that books are a lot of fun, and that within their pages are new and exciting experiences awaiting him. His appetite is thus whetted for discovering the meaning of printed symbols.

Occasionally, when a child asks questions about something, the teacher will go to a book and, through pictures and a story, help the child discover the answer. In this way she is helping him to understand that besides just enjoying books we can get information we need from them.

Reading to the child also affords him opportunities to express his creative imagination. Sometimes while reading a story the teacher may pause and ask some such appropriate question as: "What do you suppose happened then?" or "How do you think Butch felt about it?" or "What would you do?"

As the child listens to stories and watches the teacher reading to the group, he begins to associate language with symbols and pictures.

Helen Heffernan says, with regard to stimulating an interest in reading in the young child:

"The good teacher fosters esthetic enjoyment in countless situations, but again and again she will turn to the right book or story to enhance or crystallize a group experience, to afford outlet for mood or emotion, to intensify a new interest.

"It is through such functional beginnings that children learn to delight in literature. Thus before they can read for themselves they taste the satisfaction of adventuring imaginatively within the covers of a book, a taste which sometimes whets an insatiable appetite of lifelong duration."[6]

The observant, curious young child begins to notice such signs as "stop," "go," "hot," "cold," "push," "pull," and to ask, "What does it say?" He begins to "read" the names of his favorite breakfast cereals, the signs on the filling stations his parents patronize, the names of his favorite TV programs, and such magazine advertisements as Coca Cola, Camels, and others.

Toward the end of the kindergarten year the teacher may make a large but simple rebus chart of kindergarten news. There will be *no* attempt at teaching reading, but as the child associates ideas with print and pictures and watches the teacher read from left to right, he is gaining some very important basic concepts.

Learning to properly care for and appreciate books is an important aspect of the child's pre-reading experiences. As he looks at books, he gains skill in turning pages and handling them carefully. But of greatest importance to his attitude toward books and his appreciation of them is the teacher's own use of books in the group. Mabel Culkin makes this observation:

"An affectionate respect for a beautiful book . . . is an attitude in every way desirable and one which may continue throughout school life. . . . The teacher's pleasure and regard for a fresh new edition is contagious, and children learn through observation and practice to love and care for books."[7]

The kindergarten teacher realizes full well that the task of guiding the growing kindergarten child is one necessitating a team—a wise teacher and wise parents—working together for the best interests of each child and of the kindergarten group as a whole.

As she works with parents, the teacher will help them to understand the informal approach and why it is used in the kindergarten. She will help them become more aware of the expectancies for five-year-olds that are in line with their developmental level. She will interpret to parents, along through the year, the meaning of the "readiness concept," and will help them in their understanding of a wise, worthwhile program for children before they are ready for formal reading experiences.

Bibliography

Betts, Emmett A., *Foundations of Reading Instruction*. New York: American Book Co., 1950.

Burton, William H., *The Guidance of Learning Activities*. New York: Appleton-Century-Crofts, Inc., 1952.

Culkin, Mabel L., *Teaching the Youngest*. New York: The Macmillan Company, 1949.

Curriculum Guide for Baltimore Public Schools, *Living and Learning in the Kindergarten*, 1954.

Curriculum Guide for Teachers of Kindergarten. Tulsa, Oklahoma, 1955.

Dolch, Edward W., *Teaching Primary Reading*. Champaign, Ill.: Garrard Press, 1950.

Forest, Ilse, *Early Years at School*. New York: McGraw-Hill Book Co., 1949.

Foster, Josephine and Headley, Neith, *Education in the Kindergarten*. New York: American Book Co., 1948, revised 1959.

Gans, Roma, *et al., Teaching Young Children*. New York: World Book Co., 1952.

Heffernan, Helen, *Guiding the Young Child*. Boston: D. C. Heath & Company, 1951, 2nd edition 1959.

Hymes, James L., Jr., *Before the Child Reads*. Evanston, Ill.: Row, Peterson & Company, 1958.

Sheehy, Emma D., *The Fives and Sixes Go to School*. New York: Henry Holt & Co., Inc., 1954.

Stephens, Ada Dawson, *Providing Developmental Experiences for Young Children*. New York: Teacher's College, Columbia University, 1952.

Wills, Clarice and Stegeman, William, *Living in the Kindergarten*. Chicago: Follett Publishing Company, 1956.

Witty, Paul, *Helping Children Read Better*. Science Research Associates, 1950.

Chapter VIII

Guiding the Religious Development of Young Children

Day-by-Day Christian Living with Young Children

Teachers in the church's weekday educational programs for young children are frequently confronted by questioning parents who are honestly seeking to know specifically what guidance is given for the religious development of their youngsters in the daily program. Such was the case of a young mother who observed in the kindergarten one morning. During the conference which followed she commented to the teacher, "I'm interested in knowing more about the religious training the children are getting in the program here. I notice you did not tell a Bible story this morning."

One parent-teacher conference could not suffice for helping this parent understand the methods employed and the provision made for worship and other experiences which promote spiritual growth and development of the young children. The teacher will use all means at her disposal to acquaint the parents with her efforts in this area through individual conferences, group conferences, parent study groups, general parents' meetings, and the printed word.

First of all, the teacher needs to feel secure and comfortable in her entire program. She need not feel guilty or defensive when approached about her seeming lack of the use of Bible stories with the children. She understands that for the nursery and kindergarten age child there are very few Bible stories which are within the young child's capacity to understand and appreciate. She realizes that it is of greater importance to the young child for the teacher's attitudes to reflect her own relationship to God, to other persons, and to material things about her. She knows that it is in the adult's way of living his own life in and with the group that the revelation of God first comes to the child. The teacher is aware that as she knows herself as a child of God who acknowledges her finiteness and her dependence upon God's power and grace for her own life, she is helping make it possible for the child to transfer his dependence from her to God, upon whom she depends.

In the day-by-day living in the schoolroom the teacher is creating a "context of faith" for the child. She appreciates and accepts warmly and sincerely each child as he is, and she gives him the assurance of her love and concern for him. She provides a room in which he may enjoy many kinds of experiences, using equipment that is just his size and materials that interest and challenge him. She helps him feel at home and gives him freedom within limits to express his feelings and discover new meanings for himself. She will use a few Bible selections, songs, some simple refrains from great hymns of the church, prayer, pictures, and stories, as well as firsthand experiences, to enrich the child's living in the group and lift him beyond where he is at the time.

The teacher will exercise care in the arrangement of the room and in the orderliness and sequence of her time guide of the daily program. This dependability which the child senses as a result of such planning adds to his feeling of security and helps him to accept the orderliness of the universe more easily.

In providing opportunities for the child to care for materials and equipment, for personal possessions and personal routines, the teacher offers the child experiences which are the beginnings of stewardship.

By including experiences that expand the child's world and stimulate his questions about the meaning of life around him, the teacher can help him to become more aware of the "spiritual aspects" of life. As he comes to recognize evidences of God's loving care, he is enabled to experience times of true worship. When the child asks, "What does that mean?", the teacher has the opportunity to answer the question, tell a story in its natural setting, show appropriate pictures, and give the Christian interpretation in a way that has meaning for the child. The young child first learns theological truths through experience. Later, after varied and rich experiences, these truths can begin to be meaningfully verbalized for him.

Trust and obedience, which are basic elements of the Christian faith, may be developed in the young child long before he begins to understand a "system of beliefs and ethics."

Trust is developed nonverbally by structuring an environment in which the child may trust and be trusted. Without such a relationship the child may be able to verbalize glibly about God, but he will find difficulty in attaining a deep and abiding faith in God and the meaning of life in Christ our Saviour. A child's ability to put his trust in God is first dependent upon his personal relationship with some adults whom he trusts implicitly.

Obedience is taught situationally by establishing necessary limits for the child and by providing an authority which is *consistent* and tempered by grace. Meeting situations that arise from these limits may well serve to introduce the child to the righteousness of God and the orderliness of His creation. At the same time, the teacher must surround the child with loving acceptance which in a measure reflects for him the grace of God.

A teacher of young children may rightly feel that one of her most important responsibilities is to offer herself to the child as a person who trusts God's love and who can, in return, *be trusted to love the child no matter what he may say or do.* So great is this responsibility that she continually seeks divine help. The following prayer-poem from a great teacher and lover of children expresses what may well be the feelings of teachers of young children everywhere:

"If I had seen Thee, Master,
  With children on Thy knee,
And heard Thy loving accents,
  'Let children come to me,'
I think the inspiration
  Would last through all my days;
I'd speak, they'd follow after;
  They'd speak, I'd walk their ways.
O Master, fill my being
  With grace that comes from Thee;
And draw my little children
  To Thyself through me."
                        —Elizabeth McE. Shields

The Bible and Young Children

The day-by-day experiences in the weekday program for nursery and kindergarten children provide the opportunity of a laboratory for Christian living in which the Bible has the central place under the wise guidance of well-informed, Christian teachers.

Essentially the Bible is an adult book, but its message is for everyone. "The gospel news that God wants every person to be in his family, to live with him and with one another, is the gospel for every kind of person."[1]

The Bible is present in the room and comes into the young child's consciousness in many different ways as "data for the later understanding of a faith which is now being developed through relationships."[2] A beautiful large Bible is always in a prominent place, available to the children at any time. It has a place with other books but it is a very special book. The Bible in the church sanctuary is not only on the pulpit but also in the lovely stained-glass windows. It is present in the school environment in art—pictures which illustrate some of the Bible stories and incidents that are used with the children. The Bible is evident in the special days which the church celebrates, such as Thanksgiving, Christmas, and Easter. It is present in each session in conversations and in the interpersonal relationships of the children with their teachers and peers and in the relationships of the teachers with other adults in the school environment.

The Bible is taught best to young children in personal relationships with parents and teachers and other adults who reflect the Bible's message of God's grace and forgiveness.

Children can sense and know that the teacher loves them and is concerned about them even when they have done wrong. They can sense the release of the burden of guilt, experience the security they need, and retain the feeling of being accepted by the teacher and the group. This is laying a basis for the understanding later of God's forgiveness. How can children understand the forgiveness of God until first they have experienced forgiveness from those with whom they are intimately associated?

Verbalization is kept at a minimum, but the adult will use words which have "windows" that take the children beyond where they now are.

There are, for the early years of childhood, a few Bible stories, such as the story of Jesus and the children, that convey the gospel message. Since the young child's attention span is very short and his chronological sense is still undeveloped, he needs short stories which may be unrelated to one another. These may be told as "once long ago" or "long ago in Bible days."

Although few Bible stories convey the Biblical message to young children in terms they can comprehend, "the central story of God's action in history is eternally relevant. Biblical doctrines such as the doctrine of creation, judgment, covenant, Christ, church, and consummation bear upon the basic needs of children as upon adults."[3]

It is imperative that the adults working with young children recognize these "Biblical doctrines as expressions of man's profoundest experiences as he meets God."[4] Although young children are unable to conceptualize and verbalize such experiences, they are sure to sense them in their relationships with adults who are well grounded in the faith.

Young children cannot comprehend the idea of "atonement," but in their daily living they should experience over and over again having another share the burden of their faults. And again, the meaning of the word "grace" is not readily grasped or verbalized, but children need daily to live and grow in an atmosphere of grace. Later, as they mature and their concepts and vocabularies are enlarged and become useful to them, they begin to get more of the Bible message from the Bible itself.

Worship with Young Children

In the day-by-day program of the church's nursery and kindergarten groups, worship should be so integrated into the activities that all of life in the group is affected by it.

Designating a set time each day as the time for "worship," while this may be necessary with adults, will in no way ensure that the young child is developing the capacity for communion with God. It is doubtful that there will necessarily be a readiness for communion with God at such specified times. There is also the danger that the teacher who tries to provide for the children's worship at some stipulated time will consider that the religious emphasis has been taken care of for the day. Recognizing that the group has heard its Bible story, sung some religious songs, and had a prayer, she may then move on to a purely secular program of activities for the children and thus miss some rich moments of worship which could so naturally emerge.

This does not mean to imply that the teacher should not plan for the worship which she hopes the group and various individuals may have during the course of each morning. She will plan *very carefully and wisely* for the worship with the needs and interests of her children uppermost in her mind, but the timing may differ according to the responsiveness of the children.

The teacher will have the room in readiness with centers of

interest "beckoning" to the children as they arrive, "Come use me; do what you will with me." In an atmosphere of freedom which she provides, the teacher will give the children many opportunities for creative expression. Throughout the morning the manner of acceptance and appreciation of the individual in the group will have definite bearing on the religious growth that takes place. In short, the total environment of each day greatly influences, in one way or another, the children's religious living and growth.

Knowing that much of the young child's worship is spontaneous and may come at any time of the morning during any type of activity, the teacher will be sensitive to the children's readiness for worship at all times. She will be alert to attitudes and aware of moments when individuals and the group can be brought into fellowship with God. It may be while a small group is gathered around a lovely picture that the teacher helps them enrich their experience and they are lifted beyond where they are with a brief comment or a prayer: "We are glad for eyes to see such a lovely picture"; or "We are glad, dear God, for friends who paint such beautiful pictures for us to enjoy."

Once when a group of four-year-olds had sung all stanzas of "Jesus, Our Friend," a child commented, "That song just makes me feel so happy." The group shared his feeling and the teacher realized this was an opportunity for expressing gratitude to God in words. Although she voiced the simple prayer, she was giving words to the children's feelings and it became their prayer: "We are glad, God, for Jesus who taught the people and made the sick ones well. We are glad He was the children's friend and is our very special friend today."

Sometimes prayer may be an outgrowth of outdoor play. On a bright, sunny spring day following days of cloudy, rainy weather, a four-year-old ran around in the play area with utter abandon, arms uplifted as if to catch every bit of the sun's rays he could. After a few moments, he ran over to the teacher who had been observing him and said to her, "I'm just so very glad for this pretty, sunny day." The teacher shared his joy and together they said thank you to God for the warm, sunny spring day which they were enjoying.

At times spontaneous worship may be experienced as a group. Such was the case when some four-year-olds seemed to feel for the first time the comfort and coolness of the shade provided by a large tree on the edge of the play area. This experience occurred after the children had been romping and playing hard one morning in late May. It was apparent that they had never before recognized the relief that shade gives to one who has been exposed to the hot sunshine for some time. As the children enjoyed the coolness, they were helped to recognize it as one of the ways in which God cares for people and the creatures of the woods. The song "We're Glad Today" expressed their gratitude as they sang, "For the cool shade, we're glad today. Thank You, God, we thank You."

During each season of the year the children have many opportunities for making new discoveries. "One of the nearest roads from the heart of a child to God is through nature. It is easy for the . . . teacher . . . to associate the song of the birds, the sunshine, the blooming of the flowers, the trees, the evening stars, with Him who created them."[5]

Young children frequently make a place for moments of worship in their dramatic play. In the home center the "play" family sits down to dinner and the "father" asks the blessing. Or as is the custom in some homes, the play family will join hands and all pray one of their rote thank-you prayers. This should not be confused with "just playing," because most of this play with the young child is "for real."

In our discussion of the worship of young children we should not overlook the importance of returning thanks to God at "juice time." The procedure may vary, but the regularity of this tends to remind the children of the providence of God, and to encourage them to express gratitude to Him. The use of a number of different graces helps to enlarge young children's prayer vocabulary. These form prayers help children express their feelings for which they do not yet have adequate words of their own. They also tend to push outward the children's range of thoughts and attitudes. "As prayers are earnestly prayed by a group of children, there is something in the group response and the appreciation of all the children which reacts on each child."[6]

There are times when things do not go so well in the group and teachers feel the need of giving the children an opportunity to identify their feelings and the causes behind them. Such was the case with a kindergarten teacher when there had been difficulties in several of the interest centers during the work-play time. She wanted the children to face up to the situation and to recognize, if possible, some of the reasons for the unhappy incidents which occurred in their work and play. She also wanted to help them to realize that when we are sorry for things we do we can tell God about it and ask Him to help us to remember the things we should do.

The teacher approached the situation with the comment to the group, "I'm wondering how you feel about our work and play time this morning?"

One of the children volunteered that it wasn't as happy as it could have been. And when the teacher asked if he could think of a reason for the group not being so happy, she was not surprised when several of the children responded: "We didn't let the other children play with us in the playhouse"; "We didn't share the little cars"; and "Some of us knocked down the block buildings that the boys were making and they didn't like it."

The teacher then acknowledged that these things which had happened had caused the unhappy feelings among the children during their play. She explained that *everybody,* big folks as well as children, finds it hard at times to do the things he knows are right to do. She went on to tell them that God wants to help us, big folks and children alike, to live happily together.

Then, suggesting that they talk to God about it, the teacher voiced a very simple prayer: "Dear God, we are sorry about the way we treated each other in our play today. Please help us to remember tomorrow to play together in friendly ways. Help us to remember to share our toys and to let our friends enjoy the things they build with the blocks. Amen."

As was previously pointed out, the teacher, as she plans for the day's activities, will make some definite provisions for occasions of worship for individuals and for the group. This will mean the wise use of Bible stories and verses, lovely pictures, songs and poems, and material from the world about them to stimulate questioning. Teachers may frequently direct conversation in the group toward a recognition of the beautiful things God has made, in hopes that there will be a worshipful response. The following is an example of such an experience: "The children and teacher had been talking about things God had made and the teacher said, 'I feel like going to the window where we may see some of these things, and speaking to God. All who feel the same way may go with me.' As a number of the children followed, she asked, 'What would you like to say?' One voice answered, 'I love You, God,' and other voices joined in."[7] Truly it was a time of meaningful worship for those four- and five-year-olds.

The teacher's planning will also include opportunities for worship from time to time as the children visit the minister in his study, go to the sanctuary to see the stained-glass windows or to hear the organist play some of their songs and other beautiful music, or to see the pulpit Bible and hear a story from it.

Once in a while the children will profit from a short, simple, formal occasion of worship, particularly if they help to plan it. It might include a simple litany with a short response such as "We thank You, God" or the Bible prayer verse, "We give thanks to Thee, O God." (Psalm 75: 1, r.s.v.)

Then, we must recognize that there are times when the wise teacher will refrain from words. She will realize the need for silence. Feelings are so important to young children and often they communicate more than words.

In the total living of the group the teacher wants the children "to feel comfortable and secure in thinking of God. . . . The teacher herself seeks to grow in her own religious attitudes and feelings. She is sensitive to the children's needs. She lives with them in a rich, comfortable environment. Together they practice Christian living, conscious of communion and fellowship with God. This kind of worship is a part of the living together—a vital part of each . . . [school] day. It helps a child who accepts easily the fact of God, to mature in his understanding of Him."[8]

Bibliography for Teachers—Religious Development of Young Children

Bro, Marguerite Harmon, *When Children Ask*. Revised Edition. New York: Harper & Brothers, 1956.
Bullock, Henry M., editor, *Before They Ask*. For parents of four- and five-year-old kindergarten children. Nashville, Tennessee: The Graded Press, 1957.
Campbell, Elizabeth W., *Security for Young Children*. Boston: Pilgrim Press, 1952.
Denominational Curriculum Materials for the Sunday Church Nursery and Kindergarten Departments. Write to the Department of Children's Work of your denomination for printed materials useful in setting up and conducting a church sponsored nursery school or kindergarten. You may wish to secure from the various denominations the current titles of the books for young children which are part of their curriculum.
Fairly, John L. and Arleene, *Using the Bible to Answer Questions Children Ask*. Richmond, Virginia: John Knox Press, 1958.
Fritz, Dorothy B., *The Spiritual Growth of Children*. Philadelphia: The Westminster Press, 1957.
Jones, Mary Alice, *Guiding Children in Christian Growth*. New York: Abingdon Press, 1949.

Jones, Mary Alice, *The Faith of Our Children*. New York: Abingdon Press, 1943.

Jones, Mary Alice, *Tell Me About Christmas*. Chicago: Rand McNally & Co., 1958. (For teacher's use only.)

Jones, Mary Alice, *Tell Me About God*. Chicago: Rand McNally & Co., 1943. (For teacher's use only.)

Jones, Mary Alice, *Tell Me About Jesus*. Chicago: Rand McNally & Co., 1944. (For teacher's use only.)

Odell, Mary Clemens, *Our Little Child Faces Life*. New York: Abingdon-Cokesbury Press, 1939.

Roorbach, Rosemary K., *Religion in the Kindergarten*. New York: Harper & Brothers, 1949.

Shields, Elizabeth McE. and Mallard, Dorothae, *Guiding Kindergarten Children in the Church School*. Richmond, Va.: John Knox Press, 1955.

Sweet, Herman J., *Opening the Door for God*. Philadelphia: The Westminster Press, 1943.

The Preschool Program Series. A packet of 14 pamphlets. Order from Office of Publication, National Council of Churches, 120 East 23rd Street, New York 10, N. Y.

Tobey, Kathrene M., *The Church Plans for Kindergarten Children*. Philadelphia: The Westminster Press, 1959.

Trent, Robbie, *Your Child and God*. Chicago: Willett, Clark & Co., 1941, revised 1952.

Venable, Mary E., *Teaching Religion in the Kindergarten*. The Division of Christian Education of the Board of Home Missions of the Congregational Christian Churches.

Children's Books

Asher, Helen D., *A Child's Thought of God*. New York: Rand McNally & Co., 1957.

Chalmers, Muriel, *Hosanna to the King*. Ill. by Elsa Anna Wood. New York: Thomas Nelson & Sons, 1938, 1946.

Chalmers, Muriel, *The Star of the King*. New York: Thomas Nelson & Sons, 1938, 1947.

Chalmers, Muriel, *Jesus, Friend of Little Children*. New York: Thomas Nelson & Sons, 1938, 1947.

Chalmers, Muriel, *The Song the Shepherds Heard*. New York: Thomas Nelson & Sons, 1938, 1947.

Claxton, Ernest, *A Child's Grace*. Photographs by Constance Bannister. New York: E. P. Dutton & Co., Inc., 1948.

Clemens, Margaret, *My Prayer Book*. Ill. by Esther Friend. New York: Rand McNally & Co., 1947.

Eberling, Georgia M., *When Jesus Was a Little Boy*. Chicago: Childrens Press, Inc., 1954.

Entwistle, Mary, *When Jesus Was a Boy*. Ill. by Elsie Anna Wood. New York: Thomas Nelson & Sons, 1934.

Hargis, Polly, *Sunday with Stevie*. Ill. by Janet Smalley. Nashville: Broadman Press, 1956.

Jones, Elizabeth B., *God Loves Me*. Anderson, Ind.: Warner Press, 1954.

Jones, Elizabeth, *Round About Me*. Anderson, Ind.: Warner Press, 1953.

Jones, Mary Alice, *My First Book About Jesus*. Ill. by Robert Hatch. Chicago: Rand McNally & Co., 1953.

Jones, Mary Alice, *Prayers and Graces for a Small Child*. Chicago: Rand McNally & Co., 1957.

Jones, Mary Alice, *God Is Good*. Chicago: Rand McNally & Co., 1957.

Lloyd, Mary Edna, *Jesus, the Little New Baby*. Ill. by Grace Paull. Nashville: Abingdon Press, 1951.

Lloyd, Mary Edna, *Jesus the Children's Friend*. Nashville: Abingdon Press, 1955.

Muller, Carolyn Edna, *God Planned It That Way*. Ill. by Lloyd Dotterer. New York: Abingdon-Cokesbury Press, 1952.

Shields, Elizabeth McE., *When I Listen to Bible Stories*. Richmond, Va.: John Knox Press, 1949.

Van Meter, Harriet D., *Hands, Hands, Hands*. Richmond, Va.: John Knox Press, 1958.

Walker, Janie, *My Bible Book*. Ill. by Dean Bryant. Chicago: Rand McNally & Co., 1952.

White, Mary Sue, *I Know Why We Give Thanks*. Nashville: Broadman Press, 1956.

Wolcott, Carolyn Muller, *God Cares for Me*. Ill. by Lloyd Dotterer. Nashville: Abingdon Press, 1958.

Wolcott, Carolyn Muller, *God Gave Us Seasons*. Ill. by Meg Wohlberg. Nashville: Abingdon Press, 1958.

Around the World Picture Books:

World Friendship Press, 257 Fourth Avenue, New York 10, N.Y.
Children and Their Pets Around the World
Children and Their Toys Around the World
Babies Around the World
Children and Their Homes Around the World

Audio-Visual Materials

Nonprojected pictures
Denominational Kindergarten Picture Sets.
Permanent pictures suitable for Kindergarten Groups:
Christ with Children. Bella Vichon
Sistine Madonna. Raphael (detail only)
Arrival of the Shepherds. La Rolle
Morning Carol. Tarrant
All on a Summer Day. Dawson
Of Such Is the Kingdom of Heaven. Elsie Anna Wood

*Projected Pictures**
Color filmstrips. Chicago: Society for Visual Education.
Bible Books for Small People Series:
When Jesus Was a Boy
The Song the Shepherds Heard
The Star of the King
Jesus, Friend of Little Children

Family Filmstrips, Inc., a division of Family Films, Inc.
Six kits for 4- and 5-year-olds: color filmstrips with record accompanying each:

Stories About Jesus for the Kindergarten
Kit No. 1—"When Jesus Was Born"
"Jesus Is Born"
"The Shepherds' Visit"
"The Wise Men Bring Gifts"
"Growing Up in Nazareth"
Kit No. 2—"Jesus, the Friend"
"The Calling of Levi"

* Available through Denominational Departments of Audio-Visual Materials.

"Jesus and the Children"
"Jesus Visits Zacchaeus"
"Jesus Visits Mary and Martha"

Stories for the Church School Kindergarten
Kit No. 1—"Stories About the Seasons"
"God's Autumn World"
"God's Care in Winter"
"Playing in the Rain"
"Picnic in the Country"

Kit No. 2—"Stories About Home and Family"
"Big Brothers Are Fun"
"When Daddy Comes Home"
"Shopping with Mother"
"A Birthday Surprise for Daddy"

"Molly Stories About Growing Up"
"The House Next Door"
"Sandpile and Trike"
"Molly's Dollies"
"Molly's Blocks"

"Donny Stories About Growing Up"
"Surprise"
"Something New"
"The Jolly-Bus"
"The Star"

Recordings

My Book Nursery Records
"Taking Turns," "Making a Garden," "The Church Bells," "David's Pet Hen."
Nashville: The Graded Press, 1949.
Sing O Sing. Songs for Kindergarten.
Album of five records. Nashville: The Methodist Publishing House. The Graded Press, 1956.
Geneva Records for the Children's Hour
For children 3, 4, 5. Two four-record albums: "My Family" and "Holidays." Philadelphia: The Westminster Press, 1958.
Christmas recordings:
Christmas Carols. Childcraft record.
Christmas Hymns and Carols. Victor Chorus, directed by Robert Shaw.

Music Books

Crain, Margaret L., *Nursery Songs and Rhythms.* St. Louis, Missouri: The Bethany Press, 1953.
Curry, W. Lawrence, *et al., Songs of Early Childhood for Church and Home.* Philadelphia: The Westminster Press, 1958.
Lloyd, Mary Edna, editor, *We Sing Together.* For Use with Kindergarten Children at Church and at Home. Nashville: The Graded Press, 1958.
When a Little Child Wants to Sing. Philadelphia: The Westminster Press, 1935.
Home and Church Songs. St. Louis, Missouri: Christian Board of Publication, 1958.

Chapter IX

Working with Parents

"Through the children, parents and teachers are brought together in one of the most vital and far-reaching of all human relationships."[1] Mutual understanding between parents and teachers and mutual respect for each other is essential in establishing dynamic, co-operative home-school relationships. Such a relationship ensures the enrichment and co-ordination of the total life experiences of the child. No child should be forced to live in two different worlds—one at home and one at school—each with different purposes, values, and expectancies.

Teachers of young children need to keep clearly in mind a few generalizations about parents:

Parents are all very much alike. They are vitally interested in their child. They usually desire the best in educational opportunities for their child. They want their child to have all the opportunities that they themselves had and those they were denied.

Parents know many things about their child and his patterns of behavior. They can help the teacher in her understanding of the child by sharing information about his reactions in the home, with strangers, with his neighborhood peers, and in other types of experiences he may have had.

Parents are also very different. There are as many different types of parents as there are children. The teacher must value the worth of each parent and establish sincere, friendly relationships between the kindergarten and the parent. The weekday nursery school and kindergarten have also the responsibility of strengthening and broadening the ties which may already exist between families and their church.

Usually parents are the most eager for help with their child soon after his birth and again at the time he begins his first school experience. The church should be alert to these special opportunities and should assure the parents of its concern and desire to join hands in making possible for their child the training and Christian nurture which are logical and continuous.

Parents need to understand the teacher, her philosophy, and her purposes. They should have faith in her ability to keep confidences entrusted to her, and should find her easily approachable, understanding, sincere, tactful, and sensitive to parents' feelings and problems.

Because of their mutual interest in the child and his development, the parents and teacher, who work as a united team, will grow in their understandings and in the effectiveness of their mutual task.

"But children are the real winners"[2] when their home and school are working together. "They have a richer, fuller, more nourishing life, in school and out, than would otherwise be open to them. They have more consistent guidance in school and out; they stand a better chance of living up to the peak of their powers."[3]

Activities for Promoting Good Home-School Relationships

Pre-Nursery–Kindergarten Preparation

Home-school relationships begin before the child is enrolled in the weekday church group. He may be a member of the Sunday church nursery or kindergarten. If so, he will probably have less difficulty making adjustments to the group. However, provision should be made for: (1) the child's visiting in the weekday school prior to enrollment; (2) a parent-teacher conference at the church; and (3) a teacher's visit to the child in his home.

The child with his parent should have an opportunity to visit in the school after school hours. This informal meeting of the teacher and opportunity for getting acquainted with the schoolroom and play area are very important to the child. It will not only arouse his interest in attending but will help to give him a greater sense of security and feeling of "at homeness" on his first day at school.

Provision should also be made by appointment for the child and his mother to visit in the school during a weekday session before he becomes a member of the group. This affords a natural learning experience for the children as they share with their guest some of their happy times together. Such an experience also paves the way for an easier adjustment into the group for the "guest." Through this observation the parent gains some insight into the school program and has some background of understanding for making the preparations necessary for the child's entrance into school. At a conference which follows, the parent should be given an application blank for the child and a physician's report blank for recording the child's health examination.

Every weekday church school should have prepared for the parents some printed material concerning the school's philosophy and its policies concerning registration, age requirements for entrance, tuition, school year, hours of school day, health requirements, insurance, transportation, marking of clothing, and mid-morning "juice time." It might include also a brief section on "What Parents Can Do to Help Their Child."

1. Share in the child's happy anticipation of going to weekday church school.
2. Arrange for the child to have a number of experiences away from home and without his parents before he enters school.
3. Give him opportunities to do simple tasks about the house.
4. Provide a place which he can use, without adult help, for hanging up his wraps and keeping his rubbers.
5. Mark his clothes with his name and help him to recognize them.
6. Provide him with clothes which are comfortable and which allow self-help.
7. Encourage good health habits in the home: use of paper hankies, covering mouth and nose when coughing or sneezing, eating proper diet, washing hands before eating, playing outdoors, and early bedtime.
8. Encourage the child to be independent in the care of his own personal needs.
9. Be sure the child has a thorough physical examination before he enters the school. Have all required immunizations taken care of well in advance.
10. Give the child opportunities for experiences with other children his age.
11. Include the child in family conversations, particularly at the table. Do not talk down to him, nor about him in his presence.
12. Provide as many rich, firsthand experiences as you can for him, such as taking a train and bus ride, or perhaps a boat ride; eating at a hotel or restaurant; going on picnics or fishing trips, visiting the zoo and seeing the circus; helping with grocery shopping and occasionally helping cook something special; watching the construction of a new house or building; going shopping for new clothes (helping to select some of his clothes); planting a small flower bed or vegetable garden.
13. Read and tell stories to the child daily. Build for him a library of good picture and story books. Limit his TV viewing.
14. Give him opportunities for experimenting with water (blowing bubbles, playing with water toys); with sand, mud, and clay; with finger paint and with large crayons and large pieces of paper (no coloring books, please!).
15. Enjoy good music with him.

Begin Home Visiting

The next important step in establishing good home-school relations is the visit the teacher makes in the child's home. Any home visit should be made by appointment, well in advance. The home's readiness for a visit from the teacher has much to do with the parents' ease and the graciousness with which they receive the teacher and enter into a friendly, profitable conversation.

The teacher's chief concern in the pre-enrollment visit should center around the child and his home environment. In her friendly visit, as she observes the child in his home setting, the teacher gains knowledge of the things that are important to him. She also sets the stage for establishing a real companionship with him and for building a warm, congenial home-school relationship.

A pastoral call by the minister of the church to the home of the new nursery or kindergarten pupil will mean much to the family. It will not only help establish better relationships between the church and the family, but it will give evidence to the fact that the weekday church nursery or kindergarten is very definitely a part of the church's total program of Christian education for young children.

Individual Conferences

The individual conference with parents should maintain a highly important place in the church weekday program because of its direct effect on the child and his development.

Usually the conference is held in the child's classroom. It should be made by appointment, should be purposeful, and should leave the parent feeling a greater measure of security in his job as a parent.

A record of all parent conferences should be kept in the child's file. The notations should be brief, but should indicate the time and purpose of the conference and any significant facts or attitudes revealed in the conference.

The following suggestions are tips for good parent-teacher conferences:

1. The teacher *must* always be willing to be a patient listener. Listening can be active, vital, and dynamic. It often communicates feelings and attitudes better than spoken words do.
2. She should encourage the parents to express themselves freely. She does this by her manner in manifesting a genuine interest and a sympathetic understanding. (This not only helps the teacher to understand how the parent feels and reacts toward the child, but it gives the parent an opportunity to talk out the problem to someone who will listen patiently, sympathetically, and with understanding. Problems have a way of shrinking in stature when they receive this type of treatment!)
3. She must exercise respect for and recognize the worth of each parent.
4. The teacher needs to be very careful never to bring other school children specifically into any parent discussion or to draw comparisons of children in any way.
5. The teacher should try never to seem hurried or restless. The parent interview is a vitally important part of her job. Her genuine interest,

friendliness, and kindly manner not only affect the home-school relationship, but will ultimately pay rich dividends in the development of the child.

6. She must always start where the parents are, accept them as they are, and, in all events, be cautious about giving advice. It is much safer to guide the parent in making the evaluation of the problem at hand. From the discussion the parent may view the problem in a different light and will be greatly encouraged if he feels that he has thought through a possible solution. At this point the teacher might then refer the parent to a book, a magazine article, or a pamphlet in which he could pursue further the study of his problem.

7. The teacher will want to avoid using "teacherish" language. Educational jargon has no place in a parent conference. Friendly, simple words that clearly communicate meanings are essential if the parents' respect and confidence are to be gained.

8. She will not be shocked at anything that is said. This is one way of showing acceptance of the parents' way of living, doing, feeling, and thinking—with never a hint of blame or condemnation for the child's parent.

9. The teacher will avoid being on the defensive about the program and procedures in the daily sessions. She should be willing to explain her purposes for the experiences she provides for the children and indicate her reasons for using certain procedures.

10. A wise teacher will refrain from asking questions. Questions may probe into something the parent would rather not disclose. Rather, the teacher's comments should be a restatement of the parent's feelings and an acceptance of them. For example, "I'm sure you must have been discouraged," or "I know quite well how you felt—just exasperated," or "Most parents feel that way at times; it's quite natural."

11. In instances when parents sincerely ask the teacher for suggestions, it is wise for the teacher to offer several suggestions. The parent then has the responsibility for choosing. Such suggestions need be objective in nature as: "I have known some parents who met such a situation by . . ." or "Other parents have found it more effective to . . ." or "On one occasion I knew of a family that met a similar problem by . . ."

12. The wise teacher will be anxious to learn *with* and *from* the parents!

Incidental or Casual Contacts

Incidental or casual contacts as parents bring their children to school in the morning can contribute to better understanding and more effective teaching. A mother may give the teacher a bit of information which will necessitate the shifting of certain activities in the day's session if she is to meet a definite need that has arisen. Or a parent's comment may be of value only in helping the teacher understand an individual child's reaction in the group on a particular day. In any event, when the teacher regards with interest and importance the casual or chance conversations with the parent, she may often realize opportunities for more effective guidance in the session.

Telephone Conferences

Occasionally, telephone conferences with parents are necessary. Although less effective than a face-to-face conference, they can usually take care of an immediate need better than written communication. The teacher's interest in a child who is absent because of illness can be shown by a phone call. Parents respond appreciatively to such thoughtfulness.

Telephone calls have their legitimate place in the teacher-parent relationship and should be respected for their contribution to better understanding and co-operation, but they should never take the place of the face-to-face conference.

Observation in the Kindergarten

Parent observation in the weekday church nursery or kindergarten is one of the tools in the home-school relations which has not been well used. Nor has it been used enough. Potentially, it is one of the most valuable means of strengthening these relations—misunderstandings by parents may be cleared up; new understandings for parents gained.

To be most helpful, the observations should be planned for in advance. Parents should visit by appointment, should remain through most of the session, and should be given some guidance in order that the observation may be purposeful. Opportunity should be made for a follow-up conference with the teacher at a time soon after the children have been dismissed. Parents need to be aware of the fact that the teacher cannot stop to converse with them during the session they are observing. *The teacher's time, attention, and vitality belong to the children during the session.* It is well to limit the number of observers to one or two parents in any one session.

A "chatty" guide about how to observe during the session may be prepared by the staff and given to the parents as they come to visit the school. The following is a type of guide which offers some sense of direction and gives purpose in their visit.

SUGGESTED GUIDE FOR OBSERVING A SESSION

Welcome to your child's "school-home." We trust you will enjoy your visit to the fullest.

Feel free to move about the group occasionally. It is the only way you can really be sure of what is going on. It is well, however, for you to keep seated as much as possible. (This helps to keep the atmosphere more relaxed.)

In order that the children may participate in their activities normally and naturally, it is best to avoid starting a conversation with them if you can. If your own child comes to you, just be perfectly natural with him. You need not prolong your conversations, but be interested in what he has to show or tell you. Don't be surprised if at first he tends to "show off." He will soon get accustomed to your being in the room with us. As you observe the children participating in the various activities of the session, you may want to look for:

1. *The varied play interests of the children*

   Do the children have sustained interest in their play activities or do they flit from one thing to another aimlessly?

2. *The interesting responses they make to music*

   Do they participate in group singing?

   Is there any evidence of creative singing while at work and play?

   Are they interested in experimenting with musical instruments and in interpreting music through rhythmic expressions?

3. *Evidences of social learnings that are taking place*

   Do the children express willingness to take turns and to share toys and work materials?

   Are they learning to work and play happily in small groups?

4. *Interest in books, pictures, and other audio-visual material*

   How do the children use the books and pictures available to them?

   Are they interested in science materials, world globe, collections, etc.?

5. *The children's conversations with one another in their small groups and their responses in the large group*

   What interesting words do the children use?

   What opportunities do individual children have to talk?

   What opportunities are there for listening—and to whom?

   What oral language habits are evidenced in their conversations?

   Do they speak clearly and distinctly in simple complete sentences?

6. *The facts of science they are learning*

What opportunities are there for experimentation? (Examples: use of magnets, prism, playing with water.)
Are children aware of the season and distinctive manifestations of it?
Are they concerned with the care of growing plants and animals?

7. *Evidences of the practice of good health habits*

Do the children have freedom to use the bathroom as needs arise?
Do they use the drinking fountain properly?
Do they wash their hands before juice time?
Do they use paper handkerchiefs independently?

8. *Responses to art materials*

Note the various art materials the children use. Note the freedom with which they create with clay, paints, blocks, colored chalk, finger paint, and crayons.
Listen to the children's conversations while they are working with the art materials.

9. *Evidences of group participation*

Note the opportunities for problem-solving in construction activities, group planning, evaluating experiences, and discovering facts of science.

10. *The types of real life experiences*

Note the variety of firsthand experiences in which the children engage—caring for plants and animals, experimenting with musical instruments, taking excursions, entertaining friends, and many other experiences.

11. *Evidences of Christian interpretations and learnings*

What experiences do the children have that stimulate a sense of wonder and awe?
How do they express an attitude of thankfulness to God?
Watch for times when their sense of love and wonder expresses itself in childlike worship.
Do they recognize God's provision for His children's needs and His care for His world?
What opportunities do the children have to express their love for Jesus, God's Son, and to feel a desire to grow like Him in work and play?
Are they interested in the Bible stories which are told in the group?
How did they show awareness of the Bible as a very special book?

12. *The joy we all have living and learning together in the nursery or kindergarten!*

What experiences of joy or satisfaction did you see?

Parent Participation

The program of the weekday church school is so extensive and varied that it offers opportunity for each child's parents to become active participants and to make a worthy contribution to its promotion through their efforts.

Each nursery or kindergarten will have its special needs which can be met most effectively by the parents of its group. It will facilitate the enlistment of co-operation if the teacher will provide a list of the types of activities which require the services of parents during the year. Parents may check the list to indicate their interests and abilities and the most convenient time for their availability.

The best time for enlisting parents' interests is at the time of the child's enrollment. For many, this will be the child's first separation from the home. If the mother, in particular, is helped to find a way in which she will be needed to help forward the program of the school, she, too, will be helped in making her new adjustment. (Indirectly the mother's adjustment affects the child's adjustment.)

From the parents' indications of activity interests, the teacher can arrange parent participation groups. There will be those who will be interested in furnishing transportation when the children take excursions. There will be some mothers who will be interested in being responsible for planning for the social activities for the parents, such as an open house, family picnic, and parents' work nights in the nursery or kindergarten. Any parents who indicate interest and ability in doing clerical work might help with "publishing" the regular school newsletters to parents. Mothers interested in helping with sewing activities may keep up the dolls' wardrobes and adapt certain adult clothes for the children's use in "dressing up." They could also remodel the daddies' discarded shirts which are contributed for use as smocks for the children.

The fathers must not be left out of the school's parent participation. There are occasional needs for renovating or making new play equipment. Fathers, too, as well as mothers have interesting hobbies and special talents which would greatly enrich the activities of the school if they are brought into its life.

Some weekday church school leaders find it most satisfactory to provide some regular plan of parent participation in the group for as many as one or two sessions a week. This, of course, is an excellent type of parent education *if the participation is limited to certain activities,* and *if there is pre-planning with the teacher for the activity,* and *a conference following it.*

There are many contributions to the whole program which a well-organized plan of parent participation will make. Children often gain new and deeper appreciation for their parents when they come to school and make some contribution to the children's experience. One day a parent brought his cello and played for the children's group. As he was playing one of the familiar songs, he overheard one little fellow commenting to another, "You know, he's just a daddy, but look what he can do!"

When parents have opportunity to participate in the kindergarten activities, not only do they enrich the group's experiences and help build up rapport between family and school, but they gain a growing understanding of early childhood and how to become more effective in dealing with their young child in the home.

Parent Group Meetings

Mothers of young children have many things in common. At least, whenever they get together and the subject gets around to their children, they usually find that other mothers are burdened with many of the same difficulties, have made some of the same mistakes, and have experienced some of the same frustrations over like behavior problems.

The teacher can capitalize on this feeling of oneness among the mothers by providing regular meeting times for consideration and discussion of topics of greatest concern to them. These discussion topics should, in all instances, be determined by the interests and needs of the parents.

The following topics are typical of the needs and interests of many parents:

1. Answering Children's Questions
2. Discipline: What? How? When?
3. Making the Grade as Dad
4. Keeping Christmas Christian
5. Jealousy, How to Cope with It
6. Helping Young Children Deal with Their Fears
7. Do Young Children Have Worries?
8. When Children Ask About God

Parents' meetings should vary in type and procedure. The lecture method should be avoided as much as possible. The time for meetings will be determined by the needs of parents. Some groups find that it is helpful to meet regularly one afternoon a month. If this becomes the pattern, it would be well to schedule at least two meetings a year when the daddies could be included. Then there are groups, also, which find it better to plan only night meetings.

Use of a wide variety of techniques will challenge the interest of parents and make for greater effectiveness of the meetings. Each of the following might be used at some time to stimulate wider participation among the parents:

Films and filmstrips
Role-playing
Puppet play
Exhibits
Tape recordings

Slides of children's experiences which interpret the program
Panel discussion or reading panel
Attending a day's session with the child

The following brief descriptions of the above techniques, along with references to resources for their use in parents' meetings, suggest something of their effectiveness in helping groups to consider their problems.

FILMS AND FILMSTRIPS

A good film or filmstrip is an excellent means for stimulating group discussion. The film provides a common basis whereby experience can be evaluated objectively. To be stimulating for parents, the film must portray problems with which they are concerned. Just any "good" film will not contribute to a successful parents' meeting.

Filmstrips (Available from Audio-Visual Departments of denominational boards and from state Departments of Mental Health, except where otherwise indicated.)

1. *No Two Alike* (B & W) record (78 rpm)
   This filmstrip combines cartoon drawings and photography in emphasizing the truth that no two persons are alike and so should be treated differently. Various age levels are shown through reactions to given situations.
2. *As the Twig Is Bent* (B & W) record (78 rpm)
   Cartoon drawings illustrate the stages in growth of John Smith from infancy to adulthood. This filmstrip is designed to help parents and teachers understand the changing relationships in a growing child's experiences.

3. *For the Record* (B & W) records (78 or 33⅓ rpm)

This filmstrip shows how Mae and Lew Perry learn to help little Billy Perry, person, to become Billy Perry, Christian—"for his sake and the world's."

4. *The Kindergarten Child and the Church*
(Children and the Church Kit. N.C.C.C.)

While this filmstrip was prepared for the Sunday kindergarten teachers, it has much to offer teachers of the weekday kindergarten.

5. *Billy Is a Kindergartener* (B & W) with guide.

This filmstrip is designed to acquaint parents and teachers with all the various types of experiences through which the church can help Billy grow religiously.

6. *A Good Day in the Kindergarten (color, sound)*

While this filmstrip pictures life in a secular kindergarten, it depicts rich experiences which 4- and 5-year-olds need.

7. *Kindergarten and Your Child*

This filmstrip is available from the Audio-Visual Materials Consultation Bureau, Wayne University, Detroit, Michigan.

8. *David's Bad Day*

This filmstrip is available from Young America Films, Inc., 18 East 41st St., New York 17, New York. This is an interesting presentation of what happens when a four-year-old becomes jealous of a new baby at home.

Films

1. *A Long Time to Grow* (35 minutes) (sound) Part I and Part II, N. Y. U. Film Library.

These are comparatively new films. Part I shows two- and three-year-olds in a college nursery school; Part II shows the four- and five-year-olds. The emphasis is on what children are like while they are growing and learning.

2. *The Terrible Twos and The Trusting Threes*

3. *The Frustrating Fours and the Fascinating Fives*

These two films were produced by the Department of National Health and Welfare, Canada. They are a part of the "Ages and Stages" series.

4. *Fears of Children*

This film shows origins of fears, stemming from a five-year-old boy's hostility toward his father. It attempts to convey understanding of how parents can deal with the fears of children.

5. *Preface to a Life*

This is a story illustrating how the child's developing personality is affected by the attitudes and actions of his family and other adults in his life. It pictures the effects of three different kinds of parental attitudes toward the everyday experiences of the growing child. The contrast emphasizes the hopeful fact that when parents help the child to develop according to his own capabilities, not expecting too much of him and not keeping him too dependent on others, he grows up to be a man capable of living a happy, satisfying life.

6. *Answering the Child's Why*

This is an Encyclopaedia Britannica Films production dramatizing life situations in which children meet both positive and negative attitudes toward their questioning. It shows the resulting effects on their developing personalities.

7. *Helping the Child Accept the Don'ts*
8. *Helping the Child Accept the Do's*

These companion films are produced by Encyclopaedia Britannica Films. They are short, each running eleven minutes. They show how the young child meets the world of Do's and Don'ts, his reactions, and the influence his acceptance plays in forming his individual personality.

Listings available from other sources

Mental Health Motion Pictures: A Selective Guide by Federal Security Agency (1952).

Motion Pictures on Child Life by Federal Security Agency, Office of Education, Washington, D. C.

Using Mental Hygiene Films by Department of Mental Health, Lansing, Michigan. Films are available from State Departments of Mental Health.

ROLE-PLAYING

This technique is growing rapidly in popularity. It is simple to "produce"; the material for the "play-acting" comes right out of people's everyday experiences.

The group is given a problem situation—one about which parents in the group have indicated their concern. The leader sets the stage for the play-acting by describing the "plot" of the situation briefly. The following is a typical situation: "Davie is a five-year-old who finds bedtime hard to accept. He tries every means possible for putting it off. Now we need someone to play the part of Davie, someone to play the part of his mother, and someone to play the part of his father."

The parents participating are playing out a *role*. They are not being themselves or any other member of their family. The actors become just *a* mother, *a* father, or *a* child. They do not plan for the skit but develop the problem situation on the spot as they play it out. And no matter how the *situation* is handled, it gives a "focus to the discussion and a reality that sets brains working overtime."[4]

PUPPETS

Hand puppets have appeal for adults as well as children. Their manipulation takes little or no skill, just occasional movements of the puppet's head and arms.

The same procedure can be followed in presenting the situation for the puppet act as is used in role-playing.

The use of hand puppets for taking a role allows the puppeteer to be a "hidden actor." A very timid person feels more secure when he can hide behind the stage. And one other advantage this technique has over role-playing is that the puppet is the one doing the talking and exhibiting the behavior—not the parent, who might otherwise fear that his remarks would label him as "that kind of person or parent."

EXHIBITS

Exhibits can serve a number of different purposes at parents' meetings. A display of children's books at a November meeting could give guidance to parents desiring suggestions for the selection of books for children at Christmas time.

An attractive arrangement of books and pamphlets for parents, relative to the purpose of the meeting, could serve to whet the parents' literary appetites for further consideration of the problem at hand. If a mimeographed bibliography with brief annotations is made available to the parents at the meeting, there is more chance that they will make an effort to follow through with some added reading.

An exhibit of raw art materials, such as clay, paints, finger paints, and blocks, and some of the children's art work displayed with them, is a means of interpreting to parents some of the creative experiences children are having in school.

COLOR SLIDES OF CHILDREN AND THEIR ACTIVITIES AT SCHOOL

Parents enjoy watching their youngsters as they work and play in their daily sessions. An observation, followed by a conference with the teacher, is by far the most effective means of interpreting the philosophy and program of the school to parents. Color slides may be of great value in showing parents some types of activities and experiences which they were not able to observe in action. Showing slides of the children living and learning in the group, along with a stimulating commentary, gives the parents a common experience of "observation" around which helpful discussions may follow.

PANEL DISCUSSION OR READING PANEL

Although the panel is overused and greatly misused, it is a technique which serves as a way of handling problems or issues about which there are differing opinions in the group.

The participants on the panel do not have prepared speeches but talk "off the cuff" very informally. The panel discussion serves to bring into the open and to identify the problem at hand. It should prepare the parents for participation in a group discussion of the subject.

A reading panel is much more like a symposium. The difference lies in the fact that the speeches are read from publications by authorities rather than given by the authors in person. This is a way of bringing authoritative material to parents in the event that it is impossible to have "top-notch" speakers for the meeting.

TAPE RECORDINGS

For small group meetings, tape recordings can be quite effective in setting the stage for a good discussion.

Sometimes the teacher would like very much to share with parents the thinking of an expert by the expert, but all too often this is impossible. However, groups have been greatly rewarded by the generosity of a speaker whose schedule would not permit a personal appearance, but who was willing to record his message on tape which can be played for the audience.

Another use of tape recordings at a parents' meeting might be that of sharing some of the experiences of the children which the teacher felt were worth recording. The tape might include a number of recordings such as experiences in music, storytelling, and group discussions.

PARENTS ATTENDING A SESSION WITH THE CHILD

Parents and children enjoy a morning of being together in nursery school or kindergarten when adequate plans for the visiting have been made well in advance. Such an experience will aid in interpreting the school program to parents and give them opportunities for better understanding and appreciating their own child. The children enjoy the responsibilities of helping their parents to have a happy time at school as they work and play together.

Previous orientation should be given the parents concerning the purpose of this visiting experience and their part in making it meaningful to all concerned. The number of parents visiting each morning should be limited to six or eight depending on the available space. The teachers will select the dates on which the parents may visit and then give them the opportunity, well in advance, to indicate their preferences of the visiting dates most satisfactory to them. The teachers may then work out the visiting schedule and notify the parents of their appointments. With proper encouragement the daddies will be as enthusiastic as the mothers for this type of meeting.

Care should be taken to ensure that the morning's activities are free from exploitation of any kind. There is no "program" or "let's show our mothers and daddies what we can do." The day is just another good day in living and learning together. The parents come with the children and enter into the children's activities with them as participants, not as observers. This will mean that the parents will wear their "school clothes," too, and don smocks and paint with the children, work with clay, play house, and build with blocks. They will join as freely and enthusiastically as the children in such responsibilities as setting the tables for juice time, pouring the juice, passing the crackers, and caring for the plants and pets in the room.

If the length of time is set for the visiting days, the parents can be definite in making necessary plans for being away from their homes and work. An hour and forty-five minutes should allow time for the parents to enjoy the free play time, story time, music activities, and mid-morning snack time with the group. Having the time set for "visiting hours" to be over will make it easy for the parents to leave and for the children to accept their leaving.

In all the planning for this parent-child experience at school, the teacher will want to safeguard against an occasional child being disappointed in expecting his parents to visit on days for which they had no appointment. A simple way for the teacher and the children to keep up with the parents' appointments would be through the use of a large calendar. The child's name may be written in manuscript on a piece of paper with the names of other children whose parents will visit on the same date. These papers on which the names appear may be of different colors to designate each of the visiting dates. (A child will then know that his parents are coming on the "blue day," "the yellow day," or perhaps on the "green day.")

If the visiting days are scheduled over a period of several weeks, with no more than two in any one week, the regular daily program of activities can be carried on without interruption and the experiences will not overstimulate the children.

Provisions for Making the Printed Word Available to Parents

Informal notes to and from parents. Notes concerning the child need to be worded very carefully, for they may be so easily misunderstood or misinterpreted. It is a wise policy to use only positive statements about the child and to avoid *ever* making comparisons with other children. Should a problem arise, it is much better to talk it over with the parent in a face-to-face conference.

Notes from each, parents and teachers, can promote better understanding of the child, increase friendliness and rapport, and build up the feeling of the need for mutual sharing in the important business of guiding and fostering the growth and development of the child.

Newsletters. The preparation and sending out of the Newsletter can be a co-operative enterprise—parents and teachers working together. It may be only a mimeographed sheet, but it has great potential for promoting good school-home relationships, especially if parents participate in the planning and clerical mechanics of "publishing" it.

These Newsletters give parents insight into the many types of activities that are provided for the children in the nursery school or kindergarten. They should be written in a chatty, informal, personal style, to help ensure their being read. They should indicate the important learnings interestingly and simply. Parents should not be overwhelmed with a special pedagogical jargon with which they are unfamiliar. Each Newsletter might include, in addition to the school news, a description of some simple activity which could easily be provided for the child in his home. It is always helpful to parents to have the names and addresses of the children who are enrolled in the school group. This information might be included with the first Newsletter of the school year.

The Newsletter is also an effective means of letting parents know of the group's need for such things as flower cuttings, cardboard cartons, men's discarded shirts, magazines, or clothes for the dress-up box. These requests should not take the form of continual begging, however, or the parents' response upon receiving a letter will be, "Well, I wonder what they want this time."

The contents of these "chatty" notes to the parents need to be varied and timely. For example, at the Christmas season a Newsletter might include a recipe for simple candy the children made at school, with the suggestion that the child might enjoy making some at home for the family's Yuletide celebration.

The Newsletter plays an important role in interpreting to parents the program provided for the children in the weekday church nursery school or kindergarten. The following is the type of information about the kindergarten which might be sent to the home early in the school session. It may be adapted to fit a similar situation for the nursery group.

KINDERGARTEN NEWSLETTER
September 25, ———

When you asked your kindergarten child what he did in school today, you more than likely received the brief answer, "Just played. That's all."

Are we just playing or are we really learning in the kindergarten? Psychologists tell us that play for the child is *his way of learning*. It is really his life. It is his *most important business*.

But you ask, "What are the kindergarten children learning?" One of the most important things we are learning is how to get along with one another. It isn't easy, you know, and we certainly won't learn all about it this year. But we are having such a good time making a beginning at it.

We are getting acquainted with new book and story friends. The book center is quite a popular place and storytime is such a delight for all of us! "Little Squeegy Bug" is one of our favorite book friends just now. "Squeegy" is a firefly, you know.

Already we have learned several new songs and found much satisfaction in experimenting with our drums and triangles, and in skipping, running, and hopping with music.

And what fun we're having with paints and clay! Most of the children have experimented with easel painting and have had some very satisfying experiences in mixing colors on the paper. Everyone has become acquainted with finger paint. It feels so gooey and good, and such interesting things happen when inquisitive little hands work with it.

Many problems arise each day. Sometimes it is an inlay puzzle that takes just "heaps o' figgurin' " to put back together. Or sometimes it is in constructing a block garage that won't tumble in on the play trucks when they are parked in it.

You see, there are so many, many things we are learning every day, but we'll tell you more in our next Newsletter.

A Bulletin Board for Exhibiting Parent Materials

A bulletin board is helpful to have in the hall or in a room near the children's rooms. It could be used to display interesting articles for parents, book jackets from new books about children, cartoons depicting children's antics, announcements of interest to all, and perhaps snapshots of the children's activities. Parents who come early for the children might spend many a profitable minute there while waiting for their child to be dismissed. As parents become more and more interested in this means of incidental parent education, they, too, will begin bringing articles and pictures to share on the bulletin board. This is a rather subtle means of whetting parental appetites for tidbits of learning in child guidance, but it can be most stimulating and rewarding.

Near the bulletin board the church might provide an attractive display of books and pamphlets on child care and training, Christian home, child development, and other related subjects. Parents might become interested in adding to this library. The following is a bibliography of periodicals, pamphlets, and books which would be helpful for the parents of children in the weekday church nursery school and kindergarten:

BIBLIOGRAPHY FOR PARENTS' USE

Periodicals

Childhood Education. Association for Childhood Education International, 3615 Wisconsin Ave., N. W., Washington 16, D. C. Monthly journal of the ACEI. Planned for those who have a concern for children. Aims to stimulate thinking rather than to advocate fixed patterns.

Child Study. Child Study Association of America, 132 E. 74th St., New York 21, N. Y. A quarterly journal of parent education.

National Parent Teacher. 600 South Michigan Bldg., Chicago, Ill. Monthly magazine of the National Congress of Parents and Teachers. Contains articles on child development from preschool to adolescence. Serves to promote best possible home-school-community relations.

Your Today's Child. 1225 Broadway, New York 1, N. Y.

Today's Health. American Medical Association, 535 N. Dearborn St., Chicago, Ill. A monthly magazine which promotes the Association's platform, part of which is "health education and health protection for every child."

Parents' Magazine. 52 Vanderbilt Avenue, New York 17, N. Y. Monthly magazine devoted to articles and materials helpful to parents of children of all ages.

Pamphlets

Parent-Teacher Series. Bureau of Publications, Teachers' College, Columbia University, New York 27, N. Y., for the following:
  Understanding Young Children, Dorothy Baruch
  Understanding Children's Behavior, Fritz Redl
  Being a Good Parent, James L. Hymes, Jr.

Discipline, James L. Hymes, Jr.
Answering Children's Questions, C. M. Hunnicut
Children in the Family—Rivals and Friends, Edith G. Neisser
Public Affairs Pamphlets. Public Affairs Committee Inc., 22 E. 38th St., New York 16, N. Y., for the following:
    Pamphlet No. 141, *Enjoy Your Child—Ages 1, 2, & 3,* James L. Hymes, Jr.
    Pamphlet No. 163, *Three to Six: Your Child Starts to School,* James L. Hymes, Jr.
    Pamphlet No. 157, *Making the Grade as Dad,* Walter and Edith Neisser
    Pamphlet No. 154, *How to Discipline Your Children,* Dorothy Baruch
    Pamphlet No. 149, *How to Tell Your Child About Sex,* James L. Hymes, Jr.
Association for Childhood Education International, 3615 Wisconsin Ave., N. W., Washington 16, D. C., for the following:
    For Parents Particularly, reprint bulletins
    Helping Children Solve Problems
    Dealing with Fear and Tension
    Helping Children Grow
    Discipline
    Parent Education in the Nursery School, Edith Norton
    Partners in Education, Muriel W. Brown
Science Research Associates, 57 W. Grand Ave., Chicago 10, Ill., for the following:
    Parents and Teachers as Partners, Eva H. Grant
    Helping Brothers and Sisters Get Along, Helen W. Puner
    Your Child's Health, J. Roswell Gallagher, M. D.
Association for Family Living, 28 E. Jackson Bldg., Suite 1313-1323, Chicago 4, Ill., for the following:
    Fundamental Needs of the Child, Lawrence Frank
    Should a Child Talk Back?, Gladys G. Jenkins
National Association for Mental Health, 1790 Broadway, New York 19, N. Y., for the following:
    You Don't Have to Be Perfect (Even if You Are a Parent), J. S. Crossman
    Significant Symptoms in the Behavior of Young Children, Lili E. Peller
Federal Security Agency, Children's Bureau, Washington, D. C., Office of Education, for the following:
    A Healthy Personality for Your Child, Bulletin No. 337.
    Preparing Your Child for School, Bulletin No. 108.
    Your Child from One to Six, Bulletin No. 30.
    Working with Parents, Bulletin No. 7.
Child Study Association, 132 E. 74th St., New York 21, N. Y., for the following:
    What Makes a Good Home?, Anna W. M. Wolf
    Understanding Children's Fears, Arline B. Auerbach
    When Children Ask About Sex, Staff
    Jealousy and Rivalry in Children, reprint of 4 articles in Child Study Magazine
New York Committee on Mental Health, 105 E. 22nd St., New York 10, N. Y., for the following:
    Avoiding Behavior Problems, Benjamin Spock
    Pound of Prevention, James L. Hymes, Jr.
    Some Special Problems of Children 2–5 Years, Nina Ridenour and Isabel Johnson
    Teacher, Listen, The Children Speak, James L. Hymes, Jr.

Bibliography

Berson, Minnie P., *Kindergarten, Your Child's Big Step.* New York: E. P. Dutton & Co., Inc., 1959.
Block, Irma E., *Off to a Good Start.* New York; Harcourt, Brace & Co., 1953.

Bureau of Elementary Education, *Teachers Guide to Education in Early Childhood.* Sacramento, California: State Department of Education, 1956.

Garrison, Charlotte and Sheehy, Emma D., *At Home with Children.* New York: Henry Holt & Co., Inc., 1943.

Hymes, James L., Jr., *Effective Home-School Relations.* New York: Prentice-Hall, Inc., 1953.

Leonard, Edith M., *et al., Counseling with Parents in Early Childhood Education.* New York: The Macmillan Company, 1954.

Read, Katherine H., *The Nursery School, A Human Relations Laboratory.* Philadelphia: W. B. Saunders Co., 1955. Chapter 13.

Wills, Clarice D. and Stegeman, William H., *Living in the Kindergarten.* Chicago: Follett Publishing Company, revised 1956. Chapters 18, 19, and 20.

Let's Evaluate

Essentials of a Good Program for Young Children

A church planning to sponsor a weekday nursery or kindergarten, or one wishing to make a study of the program for young children which it already sponsors, will find the following helpful as a starting point in considering the essentials of a good weekday program for young children:

Adequate indoor and outdoor work and play space must be provided.

Is there ample space for vigorous play and other space for centers of interest where more quiet activities may be carried on undisturbed? ("Adequate" means 35-45 square feet per child indoors and for the outdoor play area 100-200 square feet per child.)

There must be equipment and work and play materials which help the child grow and develop to his full peak of performance for his level of maturity.

Is there a variety of work materials (paints, clay, large pieces of paper, large crayons, scrap lumber, etc.) which the child may use freely to express his thoughts and feelings and through which he may find joy and satisfaction in experimenting and creating?

Does the teacher recognize the fact that patterns, models to be copied, and pictures to be "colored in" hamper the child's creativity and can even become frustrating, damaging experiences? Is there a sufficient quantity of blocks of varying sizes and shapes to stimulate creative construction and dramatic play?

Provision should be made for resource materials which stimulate the child's curiosity and expand his background of experience.

Are there a sufficient number of attractive picture and story books of interest to the young child?

Are there a variety of musical instruments available for the child to experiment freely with sound and rhythm such as drums, bells, tone blocks, triangles, cymbals, and tambourines?

Are phonograph records used to enrich the children's experiences with songs, rhythms, and the appreciation of lovely music?

Is there a "science center" which stimulates the kindergarten child's inquisitiveness and helps him find answers to his questions? (Magnets, magnifying glass, prism, rubber tubing, aquarium, locks and keys, old clock, and such other treasures as shells, rocks, seeds, bird's nest, etc.)

Are there occasional short trips planned to enable the children to gain first-hand experiences with their environment?

An outdoor play area which is an extension of the indoor play area should be provided.

Does the outdoor play area open directly off of the kindergarten room or rooms?

Is the outdoor play area fenced in to set limits for the children and to protect them?

Is there provision for some shade as well as sunshine in the play area?

Is there a paved area wide enough for two-way traffic of wheel toys? (Preferably around the edge of the play area.)

Is there a small plot of ground which can be used for gardening activities?

Are there large pieces of play equipment such as climbing apparatus, big packing boxes, barrels, ladders, balancing boards, sawhorses, large balls, wagons, wheelbarrow, and tricycles to encourage creative play and to develop further mastery of physical skills?

Is there an outdoor storage space for the above-named equipment?

Is the sandbox located so that it will be in the direct sun during part of the day? Does it have a cover to be used at night?

Adequate plans for the protection and promotion of the child's health are essential.

Is there a daily informal health inspection of each child?

In case a child shows signs of illness, is there a room where he can be isolated until someone can come for him?

Are the daily activities planned to give the child the benefits of outdoor play when weather permits? Is the room temperature carefully regulated and the child protected from drafts? (68°-70° at the child's level in the room.)

Is the bathroom located adjacent to the playroom?

Are the bathroom facilities scaled in size for young children?

Is there provision of one commode and one washbasin for each eight children enrolled?

Are the children free to use the bathroom as their personal needs arise?

Is the drinking fountain of the projection type?

Does the lighting measure from 20-40 foot-candle light in all areas of the room? Is the light well diffused?

Do the children have individual mats on which to rest and a small, thin blanket to use as a cover?

Does each child have an individual locker for his outdoor clothing and personal belongings?

Is there a first-aid kit readily available and an adult trained to administer aid as needed? Have the contents of the kit and the first-aid procedures been recommended by a physician or a local health officer?

Many natural opportunities for growth in social adjustment and for broadening social contacts should be provided.

Does the program offer experiences in which the child learns to respect the rights and feelings of others and to share and take turns happily?

Does the child learn how to stand up for himself and resolve his problems without depending on adult interference?

Is there sufficient equipment which will stimulate social growth, such as two toy telephones, playhouse equipment, several dolls, outdoor sandbox, several small cars and trucks, dress-up clothes, balls, and large blocks?

Does the program help to extend the child's social contacts through dramatic play, excursions, and resource people who visit in the school?

The young child needs a wholesome emotional atmosphere for optimum learning and growth.

Is the teacher emotionally warm in her relationship with each child?

Does the teacher help the child to have the feeling of security and belonging in the group?

Does the teacher display firmness and consistency in her work with the individual and the group? (Yet is she flexible enough to give due consideration to special individual needs?)

Does the teacher encourage the child to express his feelings freely and naturally, whether they are socially desirable or not?

Does the teacher make sure that each child has some opportunity during the day to feel good about himself?

A good nursery school and kindergarten encourages housekeeping habits of order and cleanliness.

Are the children allowed to clean up spilled juice and the finger-paint tables?

Is there clean-up equipment scaled to child size and easily accessible to the children? (Broom, mop, dustpan, sponges, small bucket, etc.)

Is everyone expected to share in the clean-up time following the free work and play time?

Provision must be made for the safety of the group at all times.

Do the teachers keep a constant check on all equipment to eliminate all safety hazards?

Is there a fire extinguisher readily available, but not accessible to the children?

Is sand or sawdust kept around and under any outdoor climbing appartus?

Are all radiators covered to protect the child from injury?

There must be enough leadership to guide the group living and at the same time attend to the individual child's needs within the group.

Are there a leading teacher and one assistant for each 15 three-year-olds?

Are there a director or leading teacher and one assistant for each four-year-old group of 20 and one leading teacher and one assistant for each five-year-old group of 25 children?

Teachers who conduct the program for young children need to understand the young child and how he grows and develops.

Have the teachers had specialized training in early childhood education?

Have they had courses in child development, programs and group living for children under six, parent education, child psychology, and children's literature?

Do the teachers not only pay attention to what the child does, but try to determine why he acts as he does?

Do the teachers recognize each child as an individual with his own capabilities, limitations, and rate of growth?

Do the teachers have a genuine concern for meeting the individual child's needs for wholesome growth of personality rather than acting from a sentimental feeling for the "adorable little dears" and the cute things they say and do?

Teachers should recognize the importance of working with parents in the mutual task of guiding the child's physical, social, mental, emotional, and spiritual development.

Do the teachers have regular individual conferences with the parents?

Do the teachers build a feeling of "togetherness" as the parents and teachers become well enough acquainted to be relaxed and to express confidence in one another?

Do the teachers arrange for parents to observe in the kindergarten (one or two at a time only) and then follow up with a conference to interpret the activities and children's reactions?

Is provision made for parents' meetings which they help to plan and conduct? Are fathers included?

Are the teachers available after school hours for counseling with parents who may request it?

Are there at least two occasions during the year when parents, teachers, and children may enjoy a time of good fellowship together? (A seasonal party, open house, or picnic.)

It is essential that spiritual values permeate naturally the whole of the day-by-day living in the group.

Are the teachers alert to the responsiveness of the children and do they give Christian interpretations naturally as needs arise?

Are the teachers aware of the fact that for the young child the unspoken religious guidance may at times be of even greater importance than the spoken guidance?

When the questions in the foregoing evaluation form can be answered in the affirmative, it indicates that the administration and teachers are thinking and planning in terms of a good weekday church program for the young child.

Look—How They Have Grown!

The weekday church teacher concerns herself continually with evaluating the children's growth and development. (At least twice a year she will want to summarize her observations.) As she studies each child's progress, she will review carefully the file she keeps on him during the year—his medical report; his general information record; and the notations she has kept indicating the child's responses to various activities, direct quotations of the child's speech, and summaries of parent conferences about the child's out-of-school experiences.

The teacher will always be mindful of the child's oneness as a self and will realize how interrelated all the aspects of his growth are—his physical, intellectual, emotional, social, and spiritual development.

The following questions are suggested only as a guide for looking at some of the evidences of maturity at the kindergarten age level:

Physical Development

Is he regular in school attendance?
Is he learning to relax?
Does he evidence a definite handedness?
Is his posture good?
Are his toilet habits acceptable?
Can he dress himself independently, zipping or buttoning clothes?
Is he active and vigorous in his movements?
Does he have control over his large muscles (jumping, skipping, running, climbing, catching large ball, etc.)?
Does he use quiet play equipment with ease?
Does the child complain of headaches?
Does he squint, bat his eyes, or turn his head when trying to focus his eyes?
Can he discriminate likenesses and differences in objects?
Is he alert in responding to hearing games?

Intellectual Development

Can he follow simple directions?

Does he show increased ability to concentrate and to follow an activity through to completion?

Is his vocabulary adequate to communicate his experiences and retell stories?

Is he able to remember the sequence of events in a simple story?

Can he report an incident with clarity and accuracy?

Does he enjoy hearing stories?

Can he interpret what he sees in simple pictures?

Does he display an interest in language symbols?

Is he curious about his environment?

Does he enjoy imaginative play?

Can he express his thoughts and feelings through music, rhythms, and such materials as art media, blocks, and wood construction?

Does he enjoy picture-story books? Can he handle them properly?

Has he a sense of humor?

Emotional Development

Is he able to take unusual disturbances without becoming upset?

Does he have a feeling of security at home and in the kindergarten?

Does he try new things without fear of failing?

Does he meet new people without undue shyness or becoming overstimulated?

Is he able to take disappointment and defeat without crying or pouting?

Is the child free from nervous manifestations such as hair-twisting, nail-biting, or tics?

Does he have a feeling of success most of the time?

Is he happy most of the time?

Social Development

Is he friendly with his teachers and peers?

Does he participate happily in activities involving several children?

Does he accept responsibilities in group activities?

Does he take turns willingly?

Is he learning to share materials and equipment cheerfully?

Does he respect the rights and property of other children?

Is he learning to relate himself properly to the group even when it means giving up some activity he greatly desires?

Can he be a good follower as well as leader of the group?

Does he exhibit such habits of courtesy as saying "thank you" and "please"?

Is he chosen frequently by other children to share in their work and play activities?

Does he show a helpful attitude in the group?

Spiritual Development

Does he express a sense of wonder and enjoyment of the beauties of God's world?

Is he developing the ability to put himself in another's place, to understand and sympathize, and to find joy in other children's happiness?

Does he have a growing realization that God lets children help Him in the work of His world?

Is he growing in his desire and ability to express his gratitude to God?

Does his sense of love and wonder express itself in childlike worship?

Does he enjoy and know the Bible stories which have meaning for him?

Is he developing a keener sense of right and wrong, and does he desire to do right?

Does he show appreciation for the help of other people who contribute to his well-being?

Is he practicing Christian ways of living within the limits of his capacity?

Is he identifying happy times in his weekday group with his church?

Is he becoming increasingly aware of Jesus as a very special friend of little children and of all people?

The Teacher of Young Children Looks at Herself

As the teacher thinks about her responsibility for guiding young children, she will remind herself of the truth that neither the most beautiful and orderly rooms nor the finest equipment available will give assurance of effective learning. Likewise, the promotion of mental health and emotional security for young children depends on something far more than room attractiveness, functional arrangement of equipment, and modern instructional materials. This "something" is the atmosphere which the teacher creates—a wholesome emotional climate in which the children feel free to express themselves. The teacher, with her warmth of personality and self-assurance, allows reasonable permissiveness in which the children live and learn together. By "permissiveness" is meant freedom to work and play within limits which seem necessary for the welfare of the group. The teacher's acceptance of each individual child helps him to feel a sense of adequacy as well as a sense of belonging. Her unhurried manner frees the child from pressure of time. Her knowledge of each child's capacity as well as the developmental expectancies of young children guides her in the use of appropriate standards which she expects the child to meet.

Her attitude and approach with the children should be such as will establish warm, trusting teacher-pupil and pupil-pupil relationships.

In evaluating herself as a teacher, she should remember that young children *need* a teacher who:

Is in good health physically and mentally.
Is warm and sympathetic in nature.
Has clearly defined purposes.
Has a well-modulated voice.
Is calm and quiet in manner.
Is fair and consistent.
Is objective and impersonal in dealing with children's misbehavior.
Plans and prepares adequately for learning experiences which meet the children's needs and interests.
Is capable of modifying her plans when children's interests and needs justify it.
Is aware of individual as well as group responses.
Is sensitive to all that is going on in the group all the time.
Is a happy member of the group.
Has a radiant Christian personality.
Is a growing person.

The teacher needs to remember that young children *like* an adult who:

Is courteous and kindly.
Respects individuals.
Is happy and enthusiastic.
Can laugh at her own mistakes.
Has many varied interests.
Is honest with the children.
Is genuinely concerned with individual children's problems.
Is a good listener.
Has a faith in God and persons that shows.
Is attractive in manner and dress.
Has a keen sense of humor.
Can be "blind" and "deaf" at times.
Has a generous supply of praise on hand (but uses it only where it is deserved).
Helps each child to feel good about himself each day.

The following questions might serve as a guide for self-evaluation for the weekday church teacher of young children:

Do I create a classroom climate conducive to freedom of expression?

Do I maintain a balance and rhythm of active and quiet experiences during the session?

Do I continually evaluate the learning situations which I provide for the children?

Do I provide sufficient time for the children to experiment with various kinds of materials, explore and make discoveries about their environment, find satisfactory solutions to their problems, and enjoy group living?

Do I take into account in my planning and classroom procedure the individual differences in the children?

Do I co-operate with the Sunday church teachers in such matters as use of equipment, room arrangement, storage, etc.?

Do I keep myself physically fit?

Am I a happy, well-balanced individual?

Am I concerned with trying to discover the causes behind the children's behavior?

Do I use every opportunity possible for enriching the children's firsthand experiences?

Do I keep helpful individual records on each child? (Anecdotal records, samples of child's art work, etc.)

Are my relationships with the parents such that mutual benefit results from parent conferences?

Am I growing professionally? (Reading professional books and periodicals regularly, participating in local professional organizations for teachers of young children, and attending workshops or summer school.)

Do I take an active part in the life of my church, my community, my world?

Am I genuinely committed to my task of guiding young children in Christian living?

Keeping Individual Records

Record-keeping need not become a tiresome, time-consuming job for the teacher of young children if she appreciates the records for the contribution they can make to her work. A few simple records purposefully kept and intelligently used can help the teacher to better understand the child; help parents to better understand the child; indicate evidences of growth and development; indicate special needs of the child; help the teacher identify the causes of behavior difficulties; and point to needs in curriculum development.

In order to have a growing understanding of the child the teacher must have a continuous record which is kept up-to-date. She should have for each child a folder containing a health record from the child's physician, a historical record provided by the parent, brief notes of each parent conference, an anecdotal record of significant behavior, and the information from a questionnaire regarding the child's growth similar to the one given in the section entitled "Look —How They Have Grown."

Anecdotal Records

Anecdotes, if they include such things as direct quotations, descriptions of the child's activities, behavior difficulties, and emotional responses, may give a fairly continuous record of the child. These records should be brief, clear, specific word pictures of the incident. They should be dated and kept in the child's file. Comments or interpretations should be avoided.

Present progress and development can be noted, understood, and appreciated more fully in the light of the knowledge of the past.

The following are examples of anecdotal records which were kept on a four-year-old in a weekday church kindergarten:

Nov. 22—Ted experimented with finger paint for the first time. When he put blue into his yellow paint, he squealed, "Look, magic! Now I've got grass."

Nov. 26—Today Ted painted a rain picture, singing an original song and painting in rhythm to his song.

Nov. 29—Ted displayed flightiness today; did not settle down to any activity; frequently annoyed others.

Dec. 1—Ted worked with three other boys in building a big boat out of the large hollow blocks, but he didn't enter into the dramatic play with the others after the construction was completed.

Dec. 2—Ted didn't enter into any activity. He cried several times. He wanted to stay at his locker.

Dec. 3—Ted chewed the collar on his shirt or sucked his thumb most of the morning.

Dec. 4—Curling up in the doll bed with the doll's nursing bottle, Ted commented, "I want to be a baby today."

Dec. 8—Ted took the play iron from the ironing board and after "testing" it with his finger and pretending it was hot, took the doll, lifted its clothes and placed the "hot" iron on its body. He made a face as he said, "I'll burn her, I'll burn her!"

Dec. 15—Ted told how he was helping his mother take care of his baby sister.

Dec. 16—Ted was excited over giving his "baby" bed to his little sister—and getting a big boy's bed to sleep in.

Dec. 18—Ted played with several other children in the doll house. The baby doll was sick. Ted was the daddy who helped take care of the doll. He walked the floor with the doll, rocked it, and gave it some orange juice. He called the doctor on the toy phone about the sick doll.

From the record of the teacher's observations of Ted during the first week of December, it was evident that something was wrong. A conference with his mother on December 8 revealed the fact that Ted's six-month-old baby sister had been seriously ill for several days, requiring the parents' attention and care around the clock.

The observations of Ted during the following week gave evidence of his reaction to his parents' concerted efforts to give him the attention he needed and the feeling of being wanted and needed as a helpful member of the family.

The following are suggested as sample blanks, giving the types of blanks needed and the kind of information necessary for studying the growth and development of the individual child. These can be readily adapted for weekday church nursery school use.

APPLICATION FOR ADMISSION

Date _____

(Name of School)

(Church)

(Address)

I hereby make application for the admission of my child, _____

to the _____ Weekday Church Kindergarten and submit the following data for your information:

Child's full name _____ Sex _____

Name by which child is called _____

Present age _____ Date of birth: _____ Month _____ Day _____ Year _____

Address _____ Telephone _____

Previous school attendance _____

Physical handicaps _____

General health _____

Father's name _____

Occupation _____

Business address _____

Telephone _____

Mother's name _____
Occupation _____
Business address _____
Telephone _____
Church affiliation _____ If none, preference _____
Family physician _____
Address _____
Telephone _____
Date of desired enrollment _____
My reasons for desiring my child's enrollment in the kindergarten are:

_____
_____

I am enclosing _____ in payment of the application fee as required
by the school.
I understand that in addition to this application fee the tuition is _____
a semester payable at the time of enrollment and on the following dates,
_____ and _____.
Signed: _____

PHYSICIAN'S REPORT

Date _____

Name of child _____
General physical condition:
At present time _____
During the past year _____
Allergies:
Eczema _____   Hay fever _____
Asthma _____   Other _____
Skin infections _____
Any physical handicaps _____
Diseases (please check and give the date the child had each illness):

	Date			Date
___ Chicken pox	_____		___ Pneumonia	
___ Measles	_____		___ Typhoid fever	_____
___ Mumps	_____		___ Diphtheria	_____
___ Whooping cough	_____		___ Scarlet fever	_____
___ Influenza	_____		___ Rheumatic fever	_____
___ Ear infection	_____		___ Poliomyelitis	_____
___ Any other illness	_____			

Is the child subject to frequent colds and sore throats? _____
What operations has this child had? _____
When? _____

Has this child ever had a serious accident? _____

Nature of the accident _____ Date _____

Immunizations and Tests:

	Date		Date
Vaccination	_____	Schick Test	_____
Toxoid	_____	Tuberculin Test	_____
Whooping cough	_____	Booster	_____
Tetanus Toxoid	_____	Salk Vaccine	_____

Are there any other physical conditions or data, the knowledge of which would be helpful to the kindergarten staff in better understanding this child?

_____

_____

_____ M.D.

Physician

INITIAL INFORMATION BLANK

(Name of School)

(Address)

Date _____

Name of child _____ Sex _____

(Underline the name by which he is called.)

Age _____ Date of Birth _____

Month   Day   Year

Address _____

Telephone _____

Father's name _____

Occupation _____

Business address _____

Telephone _____

Mother's name _____

Occupation _____

Business address _____

Telephone _____

Other children in the family:

    Number of brothers _____ Ages ____ ____ ____ ____ ____

    Number of sisters _____ Ages ____ ____ ____ ____ ____

Other adults living in the family:

_____

General health of all members of family:
Mother _____ Other adults _____
Father _____ Other children _____
Church affiliation: _____ If none, preference _____
    Father _____
    Mother _____
Child's previous school attendance:
    Where? _____ When? _____
What contacts does (he, she) have with other children? _____
_____

Does (he, she) have imaginary playmates? _____
What are (his, her) dominant play interests?
    Indoors _____
    Outdoors _____
What are his general health habits connected with:
    1. Eating:
        Appetite _____ Between-meal snacks _____
        Any definite food dislikes? _____
    2. Rest:
        Bedtime _____ P.M. Time of waking _____ A.M.
        Afternoon nap _____ Time _____
        Any problems connected with sleep? _____
    3. Elimination:
        Any problem with toilet habits? _____
    4. Emotional development:
        Fears? _____
        Jealousy? _____
        Dependence on other persons? _____
        Nervous manifestations? (Nail-biting, thumb-sucking, etc.) ____

List contagious diseases your child has had. _____
_____

List any serious accidents your child has had. _____
_____

List any operations your child has had. _____
Check immunizations your child has had.
              Date   Date
Vaccination _____ Tetanus Toxoid _____
Toxoid _____ Salk Vaccine _____
Whooping cough _____
Is there any other significant information you might add which would further
contribute to a better understanding of your child and his needs? _____
_____

In case of emergency call:

Name _____ Address _____ Phone _____
In case of medical emergency, call:
(first choice) Doctor _____ Telephone _____
(second choice) Doctor _____ Telephone _____

Acknowledgments

Chapter I. The Church Plans the Weekday School for Young Children

1. *Findings of Weekday Church Kindergarten Workshop,* p. 56. Richmond: Presbyterian Board of Christian Education, 1952. Used by permission.
2. *Through-the-Week Church-Sponsored Nursery Schools and Kindergartens,* pp. 8-9. Nashville: The General Board of Education of the Methodist Church, 1956. Used by permission.
3. Katherine Read, *The Nursery School, A Human Relationships Laboratory,* p. 76. Philadelphia: W. B. Saunders Company, 1955. Used by permission.
4. By permission from *Nursery-Kindergarten Education,* by Jerome E. Leavitt, editor, p. 104. Copyright 1958. McGraw-Hill Book Company, Inc.

Chapter II. Standards for Good Nursery-Kindergarten Education

1. *Through-the-Week Church-Sponsored Nursery Schools and Kindergartens,* p. 37.
2. "The Teacher of Five-Year-Olds," in the *Portfolio for Teachers of Five-Year-Old Children,* leaflet No. 3. Des Moines, Iowa: Iowa Department of Public Instruction. Used by permission.
3. Read, *The Nursery School,* p. 115.

Chapter IV. Health Education in the Nursery-Kindergarten Program

1. Katherine E. D'Evelyn, *Meeting Children's Emotional Needs,* pp. 19-20. Englewood Cliffs, New Jersey: Prentice-Hall, Inc., 1957. Reprinted by permission of the publisher.
2. *Ibid.,* p. 18.
3. *Going to Kindergarten in Cincinnati Public Schools,* p. 7. Cincinnati: Cincinnati Public Schools, 1955. Used by permission.
4. *Ibid.*
5. Josephine Foster and Neith Headley, *Education in the Kindergarten,* p. 279. New York: American Book Company, 1948. Used by permission.
6. *The Primary Manual,* Curriculum Bulletin 95, p. 390. Cincinnati: Cincinnati Public Schools, 1948. Used by permission.
7. *Ibid.,* p. 391.
8. Slightly adapted from *About Us and Our Friends.* New York: Metropolitan Life Insurance Company. Used by permission.

Chapter V. Special Days in the Kindergarten

1. Mary Clemens Odell, *Our Family Grows Toward God,* p. 45. New York: Abingdon-Cokesbury Press, 1949. Used by permission.
2. *Kindergarten Leader's Guide,* p. 24, Presbyterian Graded Series. Richmond: Presbyterian Board of Christian Education, October, November, December, 1954. Used by permission.

3. *Kindergarten Bible Lessons,* vol. 40, no. 4, lesson 7, Presbyterian Graded Series. Richmond: Presbyterian Board of Christian Education, October, November, December, 1954. Used by permission.
4. Rosemary Roorbach, *Religion in the Kindergarten,* p. 164. New York: Harper & Brothers, 1949. Used by permission.
5. Mabel Louise Culkin, *Teaching the Youngest,* p. 54. New York: The Macmillan Company, 1949. Used by permission.

Chapter VI. The Program for Young Children (Part I)

1. Mary J. Nelson, "Music in Early Childhood," in *Music for Children's Living,* p. 11. Reprinted by permission of the Association for Childhood Education International, 3615 Wisconsin Ave., N. W., Washington 16, D. C., 1955.
2. Emma D. Sheehy, *There's Music in Children,* p. 56. New York: Henry Holt and Company, 1952. Used by permission.
3. From *The Sing and Play Book* by Ethel Crowninshield, p. 62. The Boston Music Company, Boston 16, Massachusetts. Copyright owners, 1938. Used by permission.
4. *Ibid.,* p. 52.
5. Sheehy, *op. cit.,* p. 27.
6. Beatrice Landeck, *Children and Music,* p. 12. Reprinted by permission of the Association for Childhood Education International, 3615 Wisconsin Ave., N. W., Washington 16, D. C., from *Music and Children,* 1948.
7. Natalie Cole, *The Arts in the Classroom,* p. 3. New York: The John Day Company, Inc., 1940. Used by permission.
8. Charles and Margaret Gaitskell, *Art Education in the Kindergarten,* p. 34. Peoria, Ill.: Chas. A. Bennett Co., Inc., 1955. Used by permission.
9. Viktor Lowenfeld, *Your Child and His Art,* pp. 98-99. New York: The Macmillan Company, 1954. Used by permission.

Chapter VII. The Program for Young Children (Part II)

1. Foster and Headley, *Education in the Kindergarten,* pp. 264-265.
2. Katherine T. Wessells, *The Little Golden Book of Singing Games,* p. 37. New York: Simon and Schuster, 1947. Slightly adapted. Used by permission.
3. Culkin, *Teaching the Youngest,* p. 202.
4. Paul Witty, *Helping Children Read Better,* p. 11. Chicago: Science Research Associates, 1950. Slightly adapted. Used by permission.
5. Lucille Harrison, *Reading Readiness,* p. 51. New York: Houghton Mifflin Co., 1939. Used by permission.
6. Helen Heffernan, editor, *Guiding the Young Child,* p. 130. Boston: D. C. Heath & Company, 1951. Used by permission.
7. Culkin, *op. cit.,* pp. 22, 21.

Chapter VIII. Guiding the Religious Development of Young Children

1. Unpublished paper prepared in 1958 by a special curriculum committee of the Presbyterian Church, U. S., p. 13.
2. *Ibid.,* p. 6.
3. *Ibid.,* p. 14.
4. *Ibid.*
5. Elizabeth McE. Shields and Dorothae G. Mallard, *Guiding Kindergarten Children in the Church School,* pp. 99-100. Richmond: John Knox Press, revised 1955. Used by permission.

6. *Ibid.*, p. 96.
7. *Ibid.*, p. 100.
8. Mamie Heinz, *Worship in the Kindergarten.* Division of Christian Education, National Council of Churches. Reprinted from the *International Journal of Religious Education.*

Chapter IX. Working with Parents

1. Muriel W. Brown, *Partners in Education,* p. 5. Reprinted by permission of the Association for Childhood Education International, 3615 Wisconsin Ave., N. W., Washington 16, D. C., 1950.
2. James L. Hymes, Jr., *Effective Home-School Relations,* p. 9. New York: Prentice-Hall, Inc., 1953. Reprinted by permission of the publisher.
3. *Ibid.*
4. *Ibid.*, p. 109.